M000210303

JavaScript Regular Expressions

Leverage the power of regular expressions to create an engaging user experience

Loiane Groner

Gabriel Manricks

[PACKT] PUBLISHING open source community experience distilled

BIRMINGHAM - MUMBAI

JavaScript Regular Expressions

First published: May 2015

Production reference: 1250515

Published by Packt Publishing Ltd.
Livery Place
35 Livery Street
Birmingham B3 2PB, UK.

ISBN 978-1-78328-225-8

www.packtpub.com

Credits

Authors
Loiane Groner

Gabriel Manricks

Reviewers
Andrea Barisone

Florian Bruniaux

Robert K Casto

Julio Freitas

Juri Strumpflohner

Commissioning Editor
Kunal Parikh

Acquisition Editor
Subho Gupta

Content Development Editor
Rohit Kumar Singh

Technical Editors
Bhupesh Kothari

Mrunmayee Patil

Copy Editor
Sonia Michelle Cheema

Project Coordinator
Mary Alex

Proofreaders
Stephen Copestake

Safis Editing

Indexer
Monica Ajmera Mehta

Graphics
Sheetal Aute

Production Coordinator
Conidon Miranda

Cover Work
Conidon Miranda

About the Authors

Loiane Groner has over 9 years of software development experience. In her university, she demonstrated a great deal of interest in IT. She worked as a teacher's assistant for 2.5 years for algorithms, data structures, and computing theory. She represented her university at the ACM International Collegiate Programming Contest – Brazilian Finals (South America Regionals), and she also worked as the student delegate of the SBC (Brazilian Computing Society) for 2 years. Loiane won a merit award in her senior year for being one of the top three students in her course. She had one of the highest GPAs in the computer science department, and also graduated with honors.

She has already worked at multinational companies, such as IBM. Her areas of expertise include Java SE and Java EE and also Sencha technologies (such as Ext JS and Sencha Touch). Nowadays, Loiane is working as a software development manager at a financial institution where she manages overseas solutions. She also works as an independent Sencha consultant and coach.

Loiane is also the author of *Ext JS 4 First Look*, *Mastering Ext JS* (first and second editions), *Sencha Architect App Development*, and *Learning JavaScript Data Structure and Algorithms*, all published by Packt Publishing.

She is passionate about Sencha and Java, and she is the CampinasJUG (Campinas Java Users Group) leader and an ESJUG (Espirito Santo Java Users Group) coordinator, both of which are Brazilian JUGs.

Loiane also contributes to the software development community through her blogs, which can be found at `http://loianegroner.com` (the English version) and `http://loiane.com` (the Portuguese-BR version), where she writes about IT careers, Ext JS, Sencha Touch, PhoneGap, Spring Framework, Java, and general development notes and also publishes screencasts.

If you want to keep in touch with her, you can find her on Facebook (`https://www.facebook.com/loianegroner`) and on Twitter (`@loiane`).

> I would like to thank my parents for educating, guiding, and advising me through all these years and for helping me become a better human being and professional. A very special thank you to my husband for being patient and supportive and for giving me encouragement throughout.
>
> I would like to thank Packt Publishing for this amazing opportunity to write books about the topics I really love! I'd like to thank all the people involved in the process of creating, reviewing, and publishing these books!
>
> I would also like to thank the readers of this book and the other books I have written for their support and feedback. Your feedback is very valuable in helping me improve as an author and a professional. Thank you very much!

Gabriel Manricks is a full-stack software and web developer, and a writer. He is the CTO at CoinSimple and a staff writer at Nettuts+, where he enjoys learning as well as teaching others. He also freelances in the fields of web consulting, development, and writing.

About the Reviewers

Andrea Barisone works for a leading Italian IT company and has over 14 years of experience in information technology, working on corporate projects as a developer using different technologies.

He also has strong experience in ECM systems, and he has several J2EE certifications. He has a great ability in acquiring knowledge of new technologies and exploiting this knowledge by working with different environments and technologies.

Andrea has reviewed the following books:

- *Agile Web Development with Rails 4*, Pragmatic Bookshelf
- *BPEL and Java Cookbook*, Packt Publishing
- *Learning Three.js: The JavaScript 3D Library for WebGL*, Packt Publishing
- *WebGL HotShots*, Packt Publishing
- *Automate with Grunt: The Build Tool for JavaScript*, Pragmatic Bookshelf
- Andrea has also reviewed the video *Building Applications with Ext JS*, Packt Publishing

I would like to thank my parents, Renzo and Maria Carla; my beloved wife, Barbara; and my two wonderful little children, Gabriele and Aurora, for making my life as wonderful as they do.

Florian Bruniaux is a web development project manager at E-motors, France. He is passionate about new technologies, particularly about process optimization, database conception, and software development.

He has worked for various companies, such as Aylan, a French start-up; Oxylane; and EDF, where he worked on IT projects. This included working on server monitoring systems, cross-browser applications, multidevice app conceptions, and software development.

Robert K Casto was born and raised in Columbus, Ohio, where he graduated from the Ohio State University with a computer science degree in 1995. He has worked for companies, such as Concentus, Nationwide Financial Services, Amazon.com, Cornerstone Brands, PCMS, OXXO, Walgreens, Best Buy, and TuneWiki. He now lives in Cincinnati, Ohio, where he started SellersToolbox in 2011 to help companies sell their products on Amazon.com. He has spoken at SCOE (Sellers Conference for Online Entrepreneurs), and he volunteers for the Strange Loop conference in St Louis and the Boy Scouts with his son. He has reviewed a number of books and enjoys learning about software technologies, especially those that help automate or simplify processes.

I would like to express my gratitude to my family for their patience and understanding of my work and busy schedule. I also want to thank the people I work with at SellersToolbox, who have become indispensible to its success, and the many companies I have had the privilege to work with and assist. It is very gratifying to be able to help others and become a part of their pursuits.

Julio Freitas graduated in computer science, specializing in information systems and technology; he's been a developer of web applications since 2000. He worked as a developer and Unix systems administrator in projects related to grid computing using Java and PHP. He's also worked at the Center for Weather Forecasting and the Climate Studies/National Institute for Space Research (CPTEC/INPE), Brazil, for 5 years. He currently resides in England, where he started off working at a web systems company. Now, he's involved in creating his own start-up and is acting as a full-stack web developer in projects focused on API development and security and building applications for mobile devices using the MEAN stack and Ionic.

Juri Strumpflohner is a passionate developer who loves to code, follow the latest trends on web development, and share his findings with others. He has been working as a coding architect for an e-government company, where he is responsible for coaching developers, innovating, and making sure that software requirements meet the desired quality standards.

When he's not coding, Juri is either training or teaching Yoseikan Budo, a martial art form, where he currently owns a 2nd DAN black belt. Follow him on Twitter, where his handle is @juristr, or visit his blog at http://juristr.com to catch up with him.

www.PacktPub.com

Support files, eBooks, discount offers, and more

For support files and downloads related to your book, please visit www.PacktPub.com.

Did you know that Packt offers eBook versions of every book published, with PDF and ePub files available? You can upgrade to the eBook version at www.PacktPub.com and as a print book customer, you are entitled to a discount on the eBook copy. Get in touch with us at service@packtpub.com for more details.

At www.PacktPub.com, you can also read a collection of free technical articles, sign up for a range of free newsletters and receive exclusive discounts and offers on Packt books and eBooks.

https://www2.packtpub.com/books/subscription/packtlib

Do you need instant solutions to your IT questions? PacktLib is Packt's online digital book library. Here, you can search, access, and read Packt's entire library of books.

Why subscribe?

- Fully searchable across every book published by Packt
- Copy and paste, print, and bookmark content
- On demand and accessible via a web browser

Free access for Packt account holders

If you have an account with Packt at www.PacktPub.com, you can use this to access PacktLib today and view 9 entirely free books. Simply use your login credentials for immediate access.

Table of Contents

Preface

Regular expressions are patterns or templates, which allow you to define a set of rules in a natural yet vague way, giving you the ability to match and validate text. They have, more or less, been implemented in nearly every modern programming language.

When working with any type of textual input, you don't always know what the value will be, but you can usually assume (or even demand) the format you are going to receive into your application. These types of situations are exactly when you would create a regular expression to extract and manipulate this input.

In this book, you will learn the basics to get started with a regular expression in JavaScript. We will start with the basics, passing through some special patterns and then, dive into two examples. The first one is validating a web form, and the second one is a very complex pattern to extract information from a log file. For all the examples, we will use a step-by-step approach, which will make it easier to learn and assimilate all the knowledge we've gained from this book.

What this book covers

Chapter 1, Getting Started with Regex, presents an introduction about regular expressions in JavaScript. It also shows how to develop the program that will be used to test the regular expressions used in the first three chapters.

Chapter 2, The Basics, covers the main features of regular expressions in JavaScript, which are vague matchers, multipliers, and ranges.

Chapter 3, Special Characters, dives into the special characters patterns of Regex. It covers defining boundaries for a Regex, defining nongreedy quantifiers, and defining Regex with groups.

Chapter 4, Regex in Practice, demonstrates how to develop a web form and validate all its fields using regular expressions functionalities learned since the first chapter.

Chapter 5, Node.js and Regex, explains step by step how to create a simple application using Node.JS to read and parse an Apache log file using Regex. It also demonstrates how to display the information from the log file into a friendly web page to the user.

Appendix, JavaScript Regex Cheat Sheet, presents a summary of the patterns used in regular expressions in JavaScript along with their descriptions, and a list of useful methods to test and create regular expressions.

What you need for this book

To develop the source code presented in this book, you will need any text editor of your preference and a browser (such as Chrome or Firefox).

For *Chapter 5, Node.js and Regex,* you will also need to install Node.js in your computer. All the required steps are described in the chapter itself.

Who this book is for

This book is ideal for JavaScript developers who work with any type of user entry data. The book is designed for JavaScript programmers who possess basic to intermediate skills in JavaScript regular expressions, and want to learn about these for the first time or sharpen their skills to become experts.

Conventions

In this book, you will find a number of text styles that distinguish between different kinds of information. Here are some examples of these styles and an explanation of their meaning.

Code words in text, database table names, folder names, filenames, file extensions, pathnames, dummy URLs, user input, and Twitter handles are shown as follows: "Now, let's take a look at some of these helper functions, starting with `err` and `clearResultsAndErrors`."

A block of code is set as follows:

```
123-123-1234
(123)-123-1234
1231231234
```

Any command-line input or output is written as follows:

```
npm install http-server -g
```

New terms and **important words** are shown in bold. Words that you see on the screen, for example, in menus or dialog boxes, appear in the text like this: "The following image exemplifies the match of the regular expression when given a **Text** input."

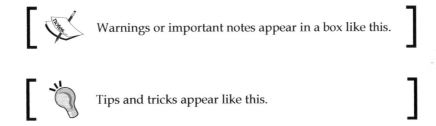

Warnings or important notes appear in a box like this.

Tips and tricks appear like this.

Reader feedback

Feedback from our readers is always welcome. Let us know what you think about this book—what you liked or disliked. Reader feedback is important for us as it helps us develop titles that you will really get the most out of.

To send us general feedback, simply e-mail feedback@packtpub.com, and mention the book's title in the subject of your message.

If there is a topic that you have expertise in and you are interested in either writing or contributing to a book, see our author guide at www.packtpub.com/authors.

Customer support

Now that you are the proud owner of a Packt book, we have a number of things to help you to get the most from your purchase.

Downloading the example code

You can download the example code files from your account at `http://www.packtpub.com` for all the Packt Publishing books you have purchased. If you purchased this book elsewhere, you can visit `http://www.packtpub.com/support` and register to have the files e-mailed directly to you.

Downloading the color images of this book

We also provide you with a PDF file that has color images of the screenshots/diagrams used in this book. The color images will help you better understand the changes in the output. You can download this file from `http://www.packtpub.com/sites/default/files/downloads/1234OT_ColorImages.pdf`.

Errata

Although we have taken every care to ensure the accuracy of our content, mistakes do happen. If you find a mistake in one of our books—maybe a mistake in the text or the code—we would be grateful if you could report this to us. By doing so, you can save other readers from frustration and help us improve subsequent versions of this book. If you find any errata, please report them by visiting `http://www.packtpub.com/submit-errata`, selecting your book, clicking on the **Errata Submission Form** link, and entering the details of your errata. Once your errata are verified, your submission will be accepted and the errata will be uploaded to our website or added to any list of existing errata under the Errata section of that title.

To view the previously submitted errata, go to `https://www.packtpub.com/books/content/support` and enter the name of the book in the search field. The required information will appear under the **Errata** section.

Piracy

Piracy of copyrighted material on the Internet is an ongoing problem across all media. At Packt, we take the protection of our copyright and licenses very seriously. If you come across any illegal copies of our works in any form on the Internet, please provide us with the location address or website name immediately so that we can pursue a remedy.

Please contact us at copyright@packtpub.com with a link to the suspected pirated material.

We appreciate your help in protecting our authors and our ability to bring you valuable content.

Questions

If you have a problem with any aspect of this book, you can contact us at questions@packtpub.com, and we will do our best to address the problem.

1
Getting Started with Regex

Regular expressions are special kinds of tools used to represent patterns syntactically. When working with any type of textual input, you don't always know what the value will be, but you can usually assume (or even demand) the format you are going to receive into your application. These types of situations arise when you create a regular expression to extract and manipulate this input.

Consequently, to match a specific pattern requires a very mechanical syntax, since a change in even a single character or two can vastly change the behavior of a regular expression and, as a result, the final outcome as well.

Regular expressions by themselves (or **Regex**, for short) are not specific to any single programming language and you can definitely use them in nearly all the modern languages straight out of the box. However, different languages have implemented Regex with different feature sets and options; in this book, we will be taking a look at Regex through **JavaScript**, and its specific implementation and functions.

It's all about patterns

Regular expressions are strings that describe a pattern using a specialized syntax of characters, and throughout this book, we will be learning about these different characters and codes that are used to match and manipulate different pieces of data in a vague sort of manner. Now, before we can attempt to create a regular expression, we need to be able to spot and describe these patterns (in English). Let's take a look at a few different and common examples and later on in the book, when we have a stronger grasp on the syntax, we will see how to represent these patterns in code.

Analyzing a phone number

Let's begin with something simple, and take a look at a single phone number:

```
123-123-1234
```

We can describe this pattern as being three digits, a dash, then another three numbers, followed by a second dash, and finally four more numbers. It is pretty simple to do; we look at a string and describe how it is made up, and the preceding description will work perfectly if all your numbers follow the given pattern. Now, let's say, we add the following three phone numbers to this set:

```
123-123-1234
(123)-123-1234
1231231234
```

These are all valid phone numbers, and in your application, you probably want to be able to match all of them, giving the user the flexibility to write in whichever manner they feel most comfortable. So, let's have another go at our pattern. Now, I would say we have three numbers, optionally inside brackets, then an optional dash, another three numbers, followed by another optional dash, and finally four more digits. In this example, the only parts that are mandatory are the ten digits: the placing of dashes and brackets would completely be up to the user.

Notice also that we haven't put any constraints on the actual digits, and as a matter of fact, we don't even know what they will be, but we do know that they have to be numbers (as opposed to letters, for instance), so we've only placed this constraint:

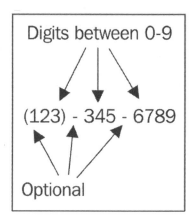

Analyzing a simple log file

Sometimes, we might have a more specific constraint than just a digit or a letter; in other cases, we may want a specific word or at least a word from a specific group. In these cases (and mostly with all patterns), the more specific you can be, the better. Let's take the following example:

```
[info]    - App Started
[warning] - Job Queue Full
[info]    - Client Connected
[error]   - Error Parsing Input
[info]    - Application Exited Successfully
```

This is an example of some sort of log, of course, and we can simply say that each line is a single log message. However, this doesn't help us if we want to manipulate or extract the data more specifically. Another option would be to say that we have some kind of word in brackets, which refers to the log level, and then a message after the dash, which will consist of any number of words. Again, this isn't too specific, and our application may only know how to handle the three preceding log levels, so, you may want to ignore everything else or raise an error.

To best describe the preceding pattern, we would say that you have a word, which can either be info, a warning, or an error inside a pair of square brackets, followed by a dash and then some sort of sentence, which makes up the log message. This will allow us to capture the information from the log more accurately and make sure our system is ready to handle the data before we send it:

$$\begin{bmatrix} \text{info} \\ \text{warning} \\ \text{error} \end{bmatrix} \text{- Log Message}$$

Analyzing an XML file

The last example I want to discuss is when your pattern relies on itself; a perfect example of this is with something like **XML**. In XML you may have the following markup:

```
<title>Demo</title>
<size>45MB</size>
<date>24 Dec, 2013</date>
```

We could just say that the pattern consists of a tag, some text, and a closing tag. This isn't really specific enough for it to be a valid XML, since the closing tag has to match the opening one. So, if we define the pattern again, we would say that it contains some text wrapped by an opening tag on the left-hand side and a matching closing tag on the right-hand side:

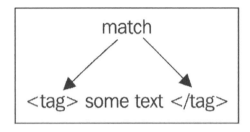

The last three examples were just used to get us into the Regex train of thought; these are just a few of the common types of patterns and constraints, which you can use in your own applications.

Now that we know what kind of patterns we can create, let's take a moment to discuss what we can do with them; this includes the actual features and functions JavaScript provides to allow us to use these patterns once they're made.

Regex in JavaScript

In JavaScript, regular expressions are implemented as their own type of object (such as the RegExp object). These objects store patterns and options and can then be used to test and manipulate strings.

To start playing with regular expressions, the easiest thing to do is to enable a JavaScript console and play around with the values. The easiest way to get a console is to open up a browser, such as **Chrome**, and then open the JavaScript console on any page (press the *command + option + J* on a Mac or *Ctrl + Shift + J*).

Let's start by creating a simple regular expression; we haven't yet gotten into the specifics of the different special characters involved, so for now, we will just create a regular expression that matches a word. For example, we will create a regular expression that matches hello.

The RegExp constructor

Regular expressions can be created in two different ways in JavaScript, similar to the ones used in strings. There is a more explicit definition, where you call the constructor function and pass it the pattern of your choice (and optionally any settings as well), and then, there is the literal definition, which is a shorthand for the same process. Here is an example of both (you can type this straight into the JavaScript console):

```
var rgx1 = new RegExp("hello");
var rgx2 = /hello/;
```

Both these variables are essentially the same, it's pretty much a personal preference as to which you would use. The only real difference is that with the constructor method you use a string to create an expression: therefore, you have to make sure to escape any special characters beforehand, so it gets through to the regular expression.

Besides a pattern, both forms of Regex constructors accept a second parameter, which is a string of flags. **Flags** are like settings or properties, which are applied on the entire expression and can therefore change the behavior of both the pattern and its methods.

Using pattern flags

The first flag I would like to cover is the **ignore case** or **i** flag. Standard patterns are case sensitive, but if you have a pattern that can be in either case, this is a good option to set, allowing you to specify only one case and have the modifier adjust this for you, keeping the pattern short and flexible.

The next flag is the **multiline** or **m** flag, and this makes JavaScript treat each line in the string as essentially the start of a new string. So, for example, you could say that a string must start with the letter **a**. Usually, JavaScript would test to see if the entire string starts with the letter a, but with the m flag, it will test this constraint against each line individually, so any of the lines can pass this test by starting with a.

The last flag is the **global** or **g** flag. Without this flag, the RegExp object only checks whether there is a match in the string, returning on the first one that's found; however, in some situations, you don't just want to know if the string matches, you may want to know about all the matches specifically. This is where the global flag comes in, and when it's used, it will modify the behavior of the different RegExp methods to allow you to get to all the matches, as opposed to only the first.

So, continuing from the preceding example, if we wanted to create the same pattern, but this time, with the case set as insensitive and using global flags, we would write something similar to this:

```
var rgx1 = new RegExp("hello", "gi");
var rgx2 = /hello/gi;
```

Using the rgx.test method

Now that we have created our regular expression objects, let's use its simplest function, the `test` function. The `test` method only returns `true` or `false`, based on whether a string matches a pattern or not. Here is an example of it in action:

```
> var rgx = /hello/;
undefined
> rgx.test("hello");
true
> rgx.test("world");
false
> rgx.test("hello world");
true
```

As you can see, the first string matches and returns true, and the second string does not contain `hello`, so it returns `false`, and finally the last string *matches the pattern*. In the pattern, we did not specify that the string had to only contain `hello`, so it matches the last string and returns `true`.

Using the rgx.exec method

The next method on the `RegExp` object, is the `exec` function, which, instead of just checking whether the pattern matches the text or not, `exec` also returns some information about the match. For this example, let's create another regular expression, and get `index` for the start of the pattern;

```
> var rgx = /world/;
undefined
> rgx.exec("world !!");
[ 'world' ]
> rgx.exec("hello world");
[ 'world' ]
> rgx.exec("hello");
null
```

As you can see here, the result from the function contains the actual match as the first element (rgx.exec("world !!")[0];) and if you console.dir the results, you will see it also contains two properties: index and input, which store the starting index property and complete the input text, respectively. If there are no matches, the function will return null:

```
> var rgx = /world/;
  undefined
> console.dir(rgx.exec("hello world"));
  ▼ Array[1] ⓘ
      0: "world"
      index: 6
      input: "hello world"
      length: 1
    ▶ __proto__: Array[0]
⟨ undefined
>
```

The string object and regular expressions

Besides these two methods on the RegExp object itself, there are a few methods on the string object that accept the RegExp object as a parameter.

Using the String.replace method

The most commonly used method is the replace method. As an example, let's say we have the foo foo string and we want to change it to qux qux. Using replace with a string would only switch the first occurrence, as shown here:

```
⟨ undefined
> str = "foo foo"
  "foo foo"
> str.replace("foo", "qux")
  "qux foo"
>
```

In order to replace all the occurrences, we need to supply a RegExp object that has the g flag, as shown here:

```
<- undefined
> str = "foo foo"
  "foo foo"
> str.replace(/foo/g, "qux")
  "qux qux"
>
```

Using the String.search method

Next, if you just want to find the (zero-based) index of the first match in a string, you can use the search method:

```
> str = "hello world";
"hello world"
> str.search(/world/);
6
```

Using the String.match method

The last method I want to talk about right now is the match function. This function returns the same output as the exec function we saw earlier when there was no g flag (it includes the index and input properties), but returned a regular Array of all the matches when the g flag was set. Here is an example of this:

```
<- undefined
> var str = "abcabc";
  undefined
> console.dir(str.match(/b/));
  ▼ Array[1]
      0: "b"
      index: 1
      input: "abcabc"
      length: 1
    ▶ __proto__: Array[0]
<- undefined
> console.dir(str.match(/b/g));
  ▼ Array[2]
      0: "b"
      1: "b"
      length: 2
    ▶ __proto__: Array[0]
<- undefined
>
```

We have taken a quick pass through the most common uses of regular expressions in JavaScript (code-wise), so we are now ready to build our `RegExp` testing page, which will help us explore the actual syntax of Regex without combining it with JavaScript code.

Building our environment

In order to test our Regex patterns, we will build an **HTML** form, which will process the supplied pattern and match it against a string.

I am going to keep all the code in a single file, so let's start with the head of the HTML document:

```
<!DOCTYPE html>
<html lang="en">
  <head>
    <title>Regex Tester</title>
    <link rel="stylesheet"
      href="http://netdna.bootstrapcdn.com/bootstrap/3.0.3/
      css/bootstrap.min.css">
    <script src="http://cdnjs.cloudflare.com/ajax/libs/jquery/
      2.0.3/jquery.min.js"></script>
    <style>
      body{
        margin-top: 30px;
      }
      .label {
        margin: 0px 3px;
      }
    </style>
  </head>
```

Downloading the example code

You can download the example code files from your account at `http://www.packtpub.com` for all the Packt Publishing books you have purchased. If you purchased this book elsewhere, you can visit `http://www.packtpub.com/support` and register to have the files e-mailed directly to you.

It is a fairly standard document head, and contains a title and some styles. Besides this, I am including the bootstrap **CSS** framework for design, and the jQuery library to help with the **DOM** manipulation.

Next, let's create the form and result area in the body:

```html
<body>
  <div class="container">
    <div class="row">
      <div class="col-sm-12">
        <div class="alert alert-danger hide" id="alert-box"></div>
          <div class="form-group">
            <label for="input-text">Text</label>
            <input
                    type="text"
                    class="form-control"
                    id="input-text"
                    placeholder="Text"
            >
          </div>
          <label for="inputRegex">Regex</label>
          <div class="input-group">
            <input
                    type="text"
                    class="form-control"
                    id="input-regex"
                    placeholder="Regex"
            >
            <span class="input-group-btn">
              <button
                      class="btn btn-default"
                      id="test-button"
                      type="button">
                        Test!
              </button>
            </span>
          </div>
        </div>
      </div>
      <div class="row">
        <h3>Results</h3>
        <div class="col-sm-12">
          <div class="well well-lg" id="results-box"></div>
        </div>
      </div>
    </div>
    <script>
```

```
    //JS code goes here
  </script>
 </body>
</html>
```

Most of this code is boilerplate HTML required by the Bootstrap library for styling; however, the gist of it is that we have two inputs: one for some text and the other for the pattern to match against it. We have a button to submit the form (the `Test!` button) and an extra `div` to display the results.

Opening this page in your browser should show you something similar to this:

Handling a submitted form

The last thing we need to do is handle the form being submitted and run a regular expression. I broke the code into helper functions to help with the code flow when we go through it now. To begin with, let's write the full-click handler for the submit (`Test!`) button (this should go where I've inserted the comment in the script tags):

```
var textbox = $("#input-text");
var regexbox = $("#input-regex");
var alertbox = $("#alert-box");
var resultsbox = $("#results-box");

$("#test-button").click(function(){
  //clear page from previous run
  clearResultsAndErrors()

  //get current values
  var text = textbox.val();
  var regex = regexbox.val();
```

```
    //handle empty values
    if (text == "") {
      err("Please enter some text to test.");
    } else if (regex == "") {
      err("Please enter a regular expression.");
    } else {
      regex = createRegex(regex);

      if (!regex) {
        return;
      }

      //get matches
      var results = getMatches(regex, text);

      if (results.length > 0 && results[0] !== null) {
        var html = getMatchesCountString(results);
        html += getResultsString(results, text);
        resultsbox.html(html);
      } else {
        resultsbox.text("There were no matches.");
      }
    }
  });
```

The first four lines select the corresponding DOM element from the page using jQuery, and store them for use throughout the application. This is a best practice when the DOM is static, instead of selecting the element each time you use it.

The rest of the code is the click handler for the submit (Test!) button. In the function that handles the Test! button, we start by clearing the results and errors from the previous run. Next, we pull in the values from the two text boxes and handle the cases where they are empty using a function called err, which we will take a look at in a moment. If the two values are fine, we attempt to create a new RegExp object and we get their results using two other functions I wrote called createRegex and getMatches, respectively. Finally, the last conditional block checks whether there were results and displays either a **No Matches Found** message or an element on the page that will show individual matches using getMatchesCountString to display how many matches were found and getResultsString to display the actual matches in string.

Resetting matches and errors

Now, let's take a look at some of these helper functions, starting with `err` and `clearResultsAndErrors`:

```
function clearResultsAndErrors() {
  resultsbox.text("");
  alertbox.addClass("hide").text("");
}

function err(str) {
  alertbox.removeClass("hide").text(str);
}
```

The first function clears the text from the results element and then hides the previous errors, and the second function un-hides the alert element and adds the error passed in as a parameter.

Creating a regular expression

The next function I want to take a look at is in charge of creating the actual `RegExp` object from the value given in the textbox:

```
function createRegex(regex) {
  try {
    if (regex.charAt(0) == "/") {
      regex = regex.split("/");
      regex.shift();

      var flags = regex.pop();
      regex = regex.join("/");

      regex = new RegExp(regex, flags);
    } else {
      regex = new RegExp(regex, "g");
    }
    return regex;
  } catch (e) {
    err("The Regular Expression is invalid.");
    return false;
  }
}
```

If you try and create a RegExp object with flags that don't exist or invalid parameters, it will throw an exception. Therefore, we need to wrap the RegExp creation in a try/catch block, so that we can catch the error and display an error for it.

Inside the try section, we will handle two different kinds of RegExp input, the first is when you use forward slashes in your expressions. In this situation, we split this expression by forward slashes, remove the first element, which will be an empty string (the text before it is the first forward slash), and then pop off the last element which is supposed to be in the form of flags.

We then recombine the remaining parts back into a string and pass it in along with the flags into the RegExp constructor. The other case we are dealing with is where you wrote a string, and then we are simply going to pass this pattern to the constructor with only the g flag, so as to get multiple results.

Executing RegExp and extracting its matches

The next function we have is for actually cycling through the regex object and getting results from different matches:

```
function getMatches(regex, text) {
  var results = [];
  var result;

  if (regex.global) {
    while((result = regex.exec(text)) !== null) {
      results.push(result);
    }
  } else {
    results.push(regex.exec(text));
  }

  return results;
}
```

We have already seen the exec command earlier and how it returns a results object for each match, but the exec method actually works differently, depending on whether the global flag (g) is set or not. If it is not set, it will constantly just return the first match, no matter how many times you call it, but if it is set, the function will cycle through the results until the last match returns null. In the function, the global flag is set, I use a while loop to cycle through results and push each one into the results array, whereas if it is not set, I simply call function once and push only if the first match on.

Next, we have a function that will create a string that displays how many matches we have (either one or more):

```
function getMatchesCountString(results) {
  if (results.length === 1) {
    return "<p>There was one match.</p>";
  } else {
    return "<p>There are " + results.length + " matches.</p>";
  }
}
```

Finally, we have `function`, which will cycle through the `results` array and create an HTML string to display on the page:

```
function getResultsString(results, text) {
  for (var i = results.length - 1; i >= 0; i--) {
    var result = results[i];
    var match = result.toString();
    var prefix = text.substr(0, result.index);
    var suffix = text.substr(result.index + match.length);
    text = prefix
        + '<span class="label label-info">'
        + match
        + '</span>'
        + suffix;
  }
  return "<h4>" + text + "</h4>";
}
```

Inside `function`, we cycle through a list of matches and for each one, we cut the string and wrap the actual match inside a label for styling purposes. We need to cycle through the list in reverse order as we are changing the actual text by adding labels and also so as to change the indexes. In order to keep in sync with the indexes from the `results` array, we modify `text` from the end, keeping `text` that occurs before it, the same.

Testing our application

If everything goes as planned, we should now be able to test the application. For example, let's say we enter the `Hello World` string as the text and add the `l` pattern (which if you remember will be similar to entering `/l/g` into our application), you should get something similar to this:

Whereas, if we specify the same pattern, though without the global flag, we would only get the first match:

Of course, if you leave out a field or specify an invalid pattern, our error handling will kick in and provide an appropriate message:

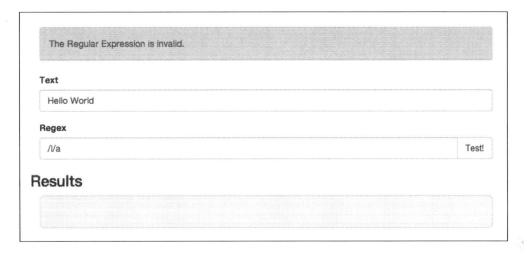

With this all working as expected, we are now ready to start learning Regex by itself, without having to worry about the JavaScript code alongside it.

Summary

In this chapter, we took a look at what a pattern actually is, and at the kind of data we are able to represent. Regular expressions are simply strings that express these patterns, and combined with functions provided by JavaScript, we are able to match and manipulate user data.

We also covered building a quick RegExp builder that allowed us to get a first-hand look at how to use regular expressions in a real-world setting. In the next chapter, we will continue to use this testing tool to start exploring the RegExp syntax.

2
The Basics

In the previous chapter, we have already seen that in order to match a substring, you simply need to write the string inside a regular expression. For example, to match `hello`, you would create this variable:

```
var pattern = /hello/;
```

We also learned that if we want to match all occurrences of the string or character of the regular expression, we can use the `g` flag within Regex. However, situations where you have as clear a pattern like these are rare, and even when they come up, it's arguable whether **Regex** is even required. You really see the true power of regular expressions when you have less concrete information.

There are two main features the Regex engine implements that allow you to correctly represent 80 percent of your patterns. We will cover these two main features in this chapter:

- Vague matchers
- Multipliers

Defining vague matchers in Regex

In this topic, we will cover **character classes** that tell the Regex to match a single vague character. Among the **vague matches**, there can be a character, digit, or an alphanumeric character.

Matching a wild card character

Let's say we wanted to find a sequence where we have `1`, and then any other character followed by `3`, so that it would include `123`, `1b3`, `1 3`, `133`, and so on. For these types of situations, we need to use a *vague matcher* in our patterns.

In the preceding example, we want to be able to use the broadest matcher possible; we can choose to put no constraints on it if we wish to and it can include any character. For these kind of situations, we have the . matcher.

A period in Regex will match any character except a new line, so it can include letters, numbers, symbols, and so on. To test this out, let's implement the aforementioned example in our HTML utility. In the text field, let's enter a few combinations to test the pattern against 123 1b3 1 3 133 321, and then for the pattern, we can specify /1.3/g. Running it should give you something similar to this:

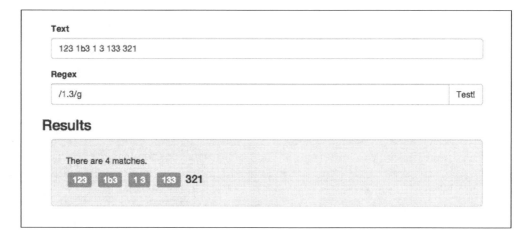

Matching digits

The **wildcard character** is not the only character to match vague patterns, nor is it always the right choice. For example, continuing from the previous example, let's say that the character in between 1 and 3 is a number. In this case, we might not care which digit ends up there, all we have to make sure of is that it's a number.

To accomplish this, we can use a \d. vague matcher The d backslash or digit special character will match any character between 0 to 9. Replacing the period with the backslash d character will give us the following results:

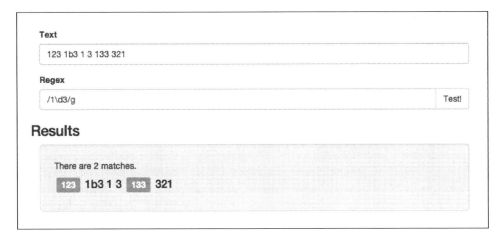

Matching alphanumeric chars

Only two out of the four matches mentioned earlier comply with the new constraint. The last main vague matcher is \w, which is a **word character**. It will match the underscore character, numbers, or any of the 26 letters of the alphabet (in both lowercase as well as uppercase letters). Running this in our app will give us the following results:

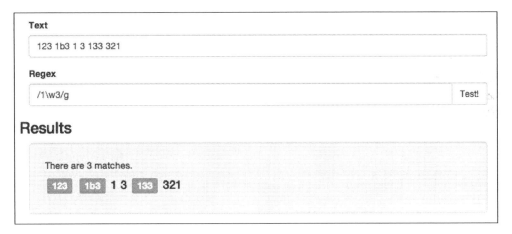

Negating alphanumeric chars and digits

Also, if you want the negated versions of the last two matchers, you can just use their uppercase counterparts. What I mean by this is that \d will match any number, but \D will match anything except a number, since they are compliments and the same goes for \w and \W.

Defining ranges in Regex

Ranges in Regex allow you to create your own custom constraints, much like the ones we just went through. In a range, you can specify exactly the characters that can be used or if it's faster, you can specify the inverse, that is, the characters that do not match.

For the sake of illustration, let's say we wanted to match only abc. In this case, we could create a range similar to [abc] and it will match a single character, which is either a, b, or c. Let's test it out with the bicycle text and the /[abc]/g pattern:

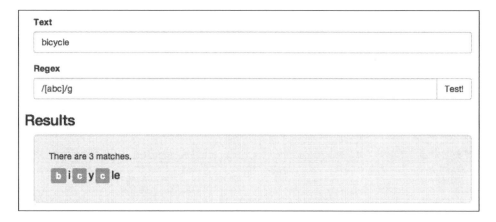

Defining a range

Now, this will work, however, if you have a lot of characters you need to match, your range will become long quickly. Luckily, Regex allows you to use the (-) dash character to specify a set of characters without needing to list them out. For example, let's say we want to check whether a three lettered name is formatted correctly, and we want the first letter to be a capital letter, followed by two lower case letters. Instead of specifying all 26 letters in each range, we can abbreviate it to [a-z] or [A-Z] for the uppercase letters. So, to implement a three letter name verifier, we could create a pattern similar to/[A-Z][a-z][a-z]/g:

Matching the dash character

If you are trying to match the dash character itself, and you don't want JavaScript to interpret it as specifying a set, you can either start/end the range with the dash character or escape it with a backslash. For example to match both "hello world" and "hello-world," we could write a pattern similar to /hello[-]world/ or / hello[\-]world/.

We can also use a wild character as a simple dot inside a rage. For example, this may occur when we want to match a number character and we don't mind having a period (forgetting for a second that a number can only have one period). So, to match 123 as well as 2.4 and .45, we could specify the /[\d.][\d.]\d/ pattern, and then both the first and second digits can be periods. Notice, JavaScript doesn't think that we are referring to the wildcard period inside the range, as this would defeat the purpose of a range, so JavaScript treats it as a standard period.

Defining negated ranges

The last thing to be covered in ranges is the **negated range**. A negated range is exactly what it sounds like. Instead of specifying what to match, we are specifying what not to match. It's very similar to adding a not (!) character to a **Boolean value** in JavaScript, in that it simply flips the return value of what you would have got earlier.

To create a negated range, you can start the range with a (^) caret character to match any character; however, for the first five letters of the alphabet, you would use something similar to /[^a-e]/.

This may not seem that useful by itself, but you might, for example, want to strip out all not alphabetical characters for a filename. In this case, you can type /[^a-z]/gi and combined with JavaScript's replace function, you can remove all of them.

Defining multipliers in Regex

Matchers are great but they only "scale" your pattern in one direction. I like to think of matchers as things that scale your pattern vertically, allowing you to match many more strings that fit into the same pattern, but they are still constrained in length, or scale the pattern horizontally. **Multipliers** allow you to match arbitrarily sized strings that you may receive as input, giving you a much greater range of freedom.

There are three basic multipliers in Regex:

- +: This matches one or more occurrences
- ?: This matches zero or one occurrence
- *: This matches zero or more occurrences

We will cover these three multipliers in this section, and also show you how to create a custom multiplier.

Matching one or more occurrences

The most basic multiplier would have to be the (+) plus operator. It tells JavaScript that the pattern used in the regular expression must appear one or more times. For example, we can build upon the formatted name pattern we used before, and instead of just matching a three letter name, we could match any length of name using /[A-Z][a-z]+/g:

This pattern represents anything that starts with a capital letter and has at least one lowercase letter after it. The plus sign will continue to repeat the pattern until it no longer matches (which in our case occurs when it reaches a space character).

Matching zero or one occurrence

The next multiplier, which I guess can be called more of a quantifier, is the (?) question mark. Fittingly, this multiplier allows the preceding character to either show up or not, almost as if we are saying that its presence is questionable. I think the best way to explain this is by looking at an example. Let's say we want to receive Apple in either its singular or plural form, for this, we could use this pattern:

```
/apples?/gi
```

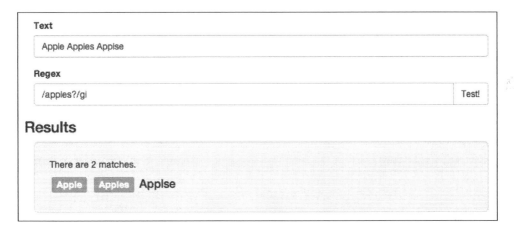

Now this may seem like the question mark is more of a conditional operator than a multiplier, but what it is really doing is saying that the preceding character can appear either once or zero times.

Matching zero or more occurrences

The next multiplier in our tool chain is the (*) asterisk. This asterisk is a combination of the previous two multipliers, allowing the previous character to appear anywhere between zero and infinity times. So, if you have an input that contains a word or a character many times, the pattern will match. If you have an input that does not contain a word or a character, the pattern will still match. For example, this can come in handy if you are parsing some kind of log for update. In situations like this, you might get update or may update!!! and, depending on the time of day, you may even get update!!!!!!!!!!!!!!!!!. To match all these strings, you can simply create the pattern /update!*/g pattern.

These are the three standard multipliers, similar to the ones that had built-in sets of characters for the (\d) ranges. Similarly, Regex allows you to specify and create your own multipliers.

Defining custom quantifiers

There is only one syntax to specify your own multipliers but because of the different parameter options available, you get three different functional options.

If you want to match a given character a concrete number of times, you can simply specify the number of allowed repetitions inside curly braces. This doesn't make your patterns more flexible, but it will make them shorter to read. For example, if we were implementing a phone number we could type /\d\d\d-\d\d\d\d/. This is, however, a bit long and instead, we can just use custom multipliers and type /\d{3}-\d{4}/, which really shorten it up making it more readable.

Matching n or more occurrences

Next, if you just want to set a minimum number of times that the pattern can appear, but don't really care about the actual length, you can just add a comma after the number. For example, let's say we want to create a pattern to make sure a user's password is at least six characters long; in such a situation, you may not want to enforce a maximum character limit, and can, therefore, type something similar to /.{6,}/:

Matching n to m occurrences

The third variation on our custom multipliers is when you want to set a complete set of options, matching both, the minimum and maximum number of occurrences. You can do this by simply adding another number after the comma. For example, if we had some sort of comment system and we wanted to constrain the comments to be anywhere between 15 to 140 characters, we could create a Regex string to match this setup, for example, /.{15,140}/.

Now, I am not saying that the two previously mentioned examples are the best uses for this kind of Regex, because obviously, there is a much easier way to check text lengths. However, in the context of a larger pattern, this can be pretty useful.

Matching alternated options

At this stage, we know how to match any set of characters using vague matchers, and we have the ability to repeat the patterns for any kind of sequence using multipliers, which gives you a pretty good base for matching just about anything. However, even with all this in place, there is one situation that has a tendency to come up and can be an issue. It occurs when dealing with two different and completely separate acceptable forms of input.

Let's say we are parsing some kind of form data, and for each question, we want to extract either a yes or no to be stored somewhere. With our current level of expertise, we can create a pattern similar to /[yn][eo]s?/g, which would match both yes and no. The real problem with this is that it will also match all the other six configurations of these letters, which our app probably won't know how to handle:

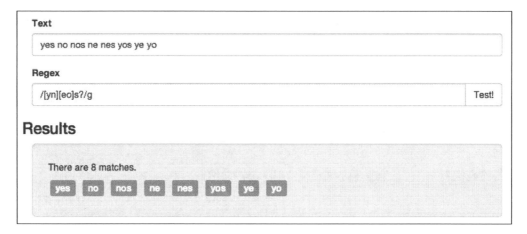

Luckily, Regex has a completely different system in place to hand situations like this and it is in the form of the (|) pipe character. It is similar to the *OR* operator you would use in an if statement, except instead of two, you just use one here. How it works is, you separate the different patterns you want to match by a pipe, and then any of the patterns can return a match. Changing our previous Regex pattern with /yes|no/g will then show the correct results:

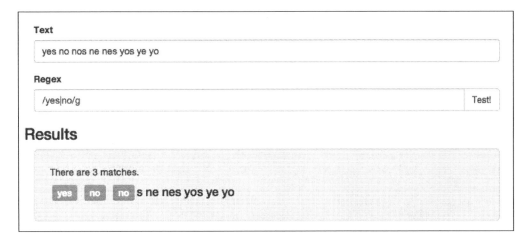

Well, at least it almost will, though it will still match no in nos. However, this is because we have been using open patterns and not really enforcing complete words (this is a topic in the next chapter).

The pipe character, though, is not limited to just two options, we can easily match a large array of values by splitting each of them by the pipe character. Also, we are not constrained to just using plain text, and each segment in our Regex split can be its own pattern using ranges and multipliers.

Creating a Regex for a telephone number

To tie up this chapter, let's put together a few of these features we just learned about and construct the phone number pattern we used in the previous chapter. To sum it up, we want to be able to match all the following number patterns:

```
123-123-1234
(123)-123-1234
1231231234
```

So, first off, we can see that there are optional brackets around the first three numbers (the area code), and we also have optional dashes between the numbers. This is a situation where the question mark character comes in handy. For the numbers themselves, we can use a built-in matcher to specify that they have to be numbers and a strong multiplier to specify exactly how many we need. The only special thing we need to know here is that the parenthesis contains special characters, so we will need to escape them (add a backslash):

```
/\(?\d{3}\)?-?\d{3}-?\d{4}/g
```

 Parentheses are used to define groups in regular expressions, this is why they are special characters. We will learn about defining groups in *Chapter 3, Special Characters*.

Testing this regular expression with the test application that we developed in *Chapter 1, Getting Started with Regex*, and with the examples mentioned at the beginning of this topic will show that the regular expression matches all of the examples:

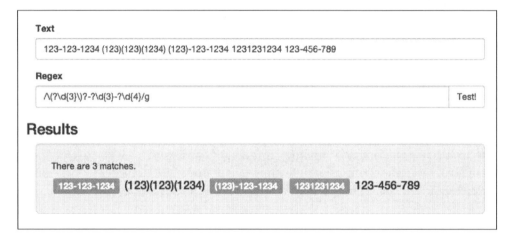

Summary

In this chapter, we learned how to use character classes to define a wild character match, a digit match, and an alphanumeric match. We also learned how to define quantifiers, which specify how many times a character or group can be present in an input.

In the next chapter, we will learn about boundaries (positions that can be used to match the Regex) and defining groups.

3
Special Characters

In this chapter, we will be taking a look at some special characters and some more advanced techniques that will help us create more detailed **Regex** patterns. We will also slowly transition from using our Regex testing environment, and go back to using standard JavaScript to build more *complete* real-world examples.

Before we get ahead of ourselves, there are still a couple things we can learn using our current setup, starting with some constraints.

In this chapter ,we will cover the following topics:

- Defining boundaries for a Regex
- Defining nongreedy quantifiers
- Defining Regex with groups

Nonvisual constraints

Until now, all the constraints we have been putting on our patterns had to do with characters that could or couldn't be displayed, but Regex provides a number of positional constraints, which allow you to filter out some false positives.

Matching the beginning and end of an input

The first such set is the *start* and *end* of string matchers. Using the (^) *caret character* to match the start of a string and the ($) dollar sign to match the end, we can force a pattern to be positioned in these locations, for example, you can add the dollar sign at the end of a word to make sure that it is the last thing in the provided string. In the next example, I used the /^word|word$/g pattern to match an occurrence of word, which either starts or ends a string. The following image exemplifies the match of the regular expression when given a **Text** input:

Using both the start and end character together assure that your pattern is the only thing in the string. For example if you have a /world/ pattern, it will match both the world string as well as any other string which merely contains world in it, such as hello world. However, if you wanted to make sure that the string only contains world, you can modify the pattern to be /^world$/. This means that Regex will attempt to find the pattern which, both, begins the string and ends it. This, of course, will only happen if it is the only thing in the string.

This is the default behavior but it is worth mentioning that this isn't always the case. In the previous chapter, we saw the m or multiline flag, and what this flag does is that it makes the caret character match not only the beginning of the string but also the beginning of any line. The same goes for the dollar sign: it will match the end of each line instead of the end of the entire string. So, it really comes down to what you need in a given situation.

Matching word boundaries

Word boundaries are very similar to the **string boundaries** we just saw, except that they work in the context of a single word. For example, we want to match can, but this refers to can alone, and not can from candy. We saw in the previous example, if you just type a pattern, such as /can/g, you will get matches for can even if it's a part of another word, for example, in a situation where the user typed candy. Using a backslash (\b) character, we can denote a word boundary (either in the beginning or at the end), so that we can fix this problem using a pattern similar to /\bcan\b/g, as shown here:

Matching nonword boundaries

Paired with the \b character, we have the \B symbol, which is its inverse. Similar to what we have seen on multiple occasions, a capital symbol usually refers to the opposite functionality, and is no exception. The uppercase version will put a constraint on the pattern that limits it from being at the edge of word. Now, we'll run the same example text, except with /can\B/g, which will swap the matches; this is because the n in can is at its boundary:

Matching a whitespace character

You can match a whitespace character using the backslash s character, and it matches things such as spaces and tabs. It is similar to a word boundary, but it does have some distinctions. First of all, a word boundary matches the end of a word even if it is the last word in a pattern, unlike the whitespace character, which would require an extra space. So, /foo\b/ would match foo. However, /foo\s/ would not, because there is no following space character at the end of the string. Another difference is that a boundary matcher will count something similar to a period or dash as an actual boundary, though the whitespace character will only match a string if there is a whitespace:

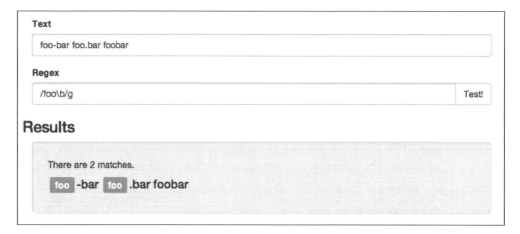

 It's worth mentioning that the whitespace character has an \S inverse matcher, which will match anything but a whitespace character.

Defining nongreedy quantifiers

In the previous section, we had a look at multipliers, where you can specify that a pattern should be repeated a certain number of times. By default, JavaScript will try and match the largest number of characters possible, which means that it will be a **greedy match**. Let's say we have a pattern similar to /\d{1,4}/ that will match any text and has between one and four numbers. By default, if we use 124582948, it will return 1245, as it will take the maximum number of options (greedy approach). However, if we want, we can add the (?) question mark operator to tell JavaScript not to use greedy matching and instead return the minimum number of characters as possible:

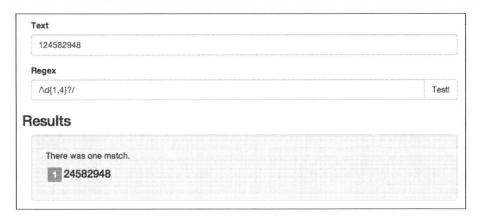

Greedy matching is something that makes it difficult to find bugs in your code. Consider the following example text:

```
<div class="container" id="main">
    Site content
<div>
```

If we wanted to extract the class, you might think of writing a pattern in this way:

```
/class=".*"/
```

The problem here is that the * character will attempt to match as many characters as possible, so instead of getting container like we wanted, we would get "container" id="main". Since the dot character will match anything, the regular expression will match from the first quotation mark before the class word to the closing quotation mark right before the id word. To fix this, we can use the ungreedy question mark and change the pattern to /class=".*?"/. This will cause it to stop at the minimum required match, which is when we reach the first quotation mark:

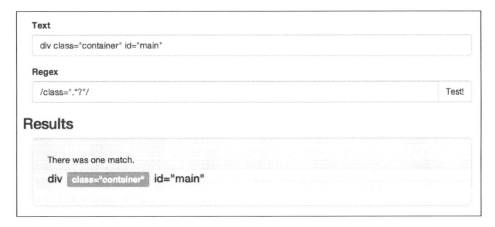

Matching groups in Regex

The last main topic that I have left out until now is **groups**. However, in order to work with groups, we have to move back into a JavaScript console, as this will provide the actual results object that we will need to look at.

Groups show how we can extract data from the input provided. Without groups, you can check whether there is a match, or if a given input text follows a specific pattern. However, you can't take advantage of vague definitions to extract relevant content. The syntax is fairly simple: you wrap the pattern you want inside brackets, and then this part of the expression will be extracted in its own property.

Grouping characters together to create a clause

Let's start with something basic—a person's name—in standard JavaScript. If you had a string with someone's name, you would probably split it by the space character and check whether there are two or three components in it. In case there are two, the first would consist of the first name and the second would consist of the last name; however, if there are three components, then the second component would include the middle name and the third would include the last name.

Instead of imposing a condition like this, we can create a simple pattern as shown:

```
/(\S+) (\S*) ?\b(\S+)/
```

The first group contains a mandatory non-space word. The plus sign will again multiply the pattern indefinitely. Next, we want a space with a second word; this time, I've used the asterisk to denote that it could be of length zero, and after this, we have another space, though, this time, it's optional.

 If there is no middle name, there won't be a second space, followed by a word boundary. This is because the space is optional, but we still want to make sure that a new word is present, followed by the final word.

Now, open up a JavaScript console (in Chrome) and create a variable for this pattern:

```
var pattern = /(\S+) (\S*) ?\b(\S+)/
```

Then, try running the `exec` command on this pattern with different names, with and without a middle name, and take a look at this resulting output:

```
> pattern.exec("John Smith");
  ["John Smith", "John", "", "Smith"]
> pattern.exec("John M. Smith");
  ["John M. Smith", "John", "M.", "Smith"]
> pattern.exec("John Mor Smith");
  ["John Mor Smith", "John", "Mor", "Smith"]
```

Whether the string has a middle name or not, it will have the three patterns that we can assign to variables, therefore, we can use something else instead of this:

```
var res = name.split(" ");
first_name = res[0];

if (res.length == 2) {
   middle_name = "";
   last_name = res[1];
} else {
   middle_name = res[1];
   last_name = res[2];
}
```

We can remove the conditional statements (`if-else`) from the preceding code and write the code something similar to this:

```
var res = /(\S+) (\S*) ?\b(\S+)/.exec(name);

first_name = res[1];
middle_name = res[2];
last_name = res[3];
```

If the middle name is left out, our expression will still have the group, it will just be an empty string.

Another thing worth mentioning is that the indexes of the groups start at 1, so the first group is in the result 1 index, and the result 0 index holds the entire match.

Capture and noncapture groups

In the first chapter, we saw an example where we wanted to parse some kind of **XML** tokens, and we said that we needed an extra constraint where the closing tag had to match the opening tag for it to be valid. So, for example, this should be parsed:

```
<duration>5 Minutes</duration>
```

Here, this should not be parsed:

```
<duration>5 Minutes</title>
```

Since the closing tag doesn't match the opening tag, the way to reference previous groups in your pattern is by using a backslash character, followed by the group's index number. As an example, let's write a small script that will accept a line delimited series of **XML** tags, and then convert it into a JavaScript object.

To start with, let's create an input string:

```
var xml = [
    "<title>File.js</title>",
    "<size>36 KB</size>",
    "<language>JavaScript</language>",
    "<modified>5 Minutes</name>"
].join("\n");
```

Here, we have four properties, but the last property does not have a valid closing tag, so it should not be picked up. Next, we will cycle through this pattern and set the properties of a `data` object:

```
var data = {};

xml.split("\n").forEach(function(line){
    match = /<(\w+)>([^<]*)<\/\1>/.exec(line);
    if (match) {
        var tag = match[1];
        data[tag] = match[2];
    }
});
```

If we output data in a console, you will see that we do, in fact, get three valid properties:

```
data;
Object {title: "File.js", size: "36 KB", language: "JavaScript"}
>
```

However, let's take a moment to examine the pattern; we look for some opening tags with a name inside them, and we then pick up all the characters, except for an opening triangle brace using a negated range. After this, we look for a closing tag using a (\1) back reference to make sure it matches. You may have also realized that we needed to escape the forward slash, so it wouldn't think we were closing the Regexp pattern.

A back reference, when added to the end of a regular expression pattern, allows you to back reference a sub-pattern within a pattern, so that the value of the sub-pattern is remembered and used as part of the matching. For example, / (no) \1 / matches nono in nono. \1 and is replaced with the value of the first sub-pattern within a pattern, or with (no), so as to form the final pattern.

All the groups we have seen so far have been **capture groups**, and they tell Regexp to extract this portion of the pattern into its own variable. However, there are other groups or uses for brackets that can be made to achieve even more functionality, the first of these is a non capture group.

Matching non capture groups

A **non capture group** groups a part of a pattern but it does not actually extract this data into the results array, or use it in back referencing. One benefit of this is that it allows you to use character modifiers on full sections in your pattern. For example, if we want to get a pattern that repeats world indefinitely, we can write it as this:

```
/(?:world)*/
```

This will match world as well as worldworldworld and so on. The syntax for a noncapture group is similar to a standard group, except that you start it with a question mark and a (?:) colon. Grouping it allows us to consider the entire thing as a single object, and use modifiers, which usually only work on individual characters.

The other most common use for noncapture groups (which can be done in capture groups as well) works in conjunction with a pipe character. A pipe character allows you to insert multiple options one after the other inside your pattern, for example, in a situation where we want to match either yes or no, we can create this pattern:

```
/yes|no/
```

Most of the time, though, this set of options will only be a small piece of your pattern. For example, if we are parsing log messages, we may want to extract the log level and the message. The log level can be one of only a few options (such as debug, info, error, and so on), but the message will always be there. Now, you can write a pattern instead of this one:

```
/[info] - .*|[debug] - .*|[error] - .*/
```

We can extract the common part into its own noncapture group:

```
/[(?:info|debug|error)] - .*/
```

By doing this we remove a lot of the duplicate code.

Matching lookahead groups

The last sets of groups you can have in your code are **lookahead** groups. These groups allow us to set a constraint on a pattern, but not really include this constraint in an actual match. With noncapture groups, JavaScript will not create a special index for a section, although, it will include it in the full results (the result's first element). With lookahead groups, we want to be able to make sure there is or isn't some text after our match, but we don't want this text in the results.

For example, let's say we have some input text and we want to parse out all .com domain names. We might not necessarily want .com in the match, just the actual domain name. In this case, we can create this pattern:

```
/\w+(?=\.com)/g
```

The group with the ?= character will mean that we want it to have this text at the end of our pattern, but we don't actually want to include it; we also have to escape the period since it is a special character. Now, we can use this pattern to extract the domains:

```
text.match(/\w+(?=\.com)/g)
```

We can assume that we have a variable text similar to this:

```
> var text = "Bookmarks: http://google.com http://tutsplus.com http://twitter.com"
  undefined
> text.match(/\w+(?=\.com)/g)
  ["google", "tutsplus", "twitter"]
>
```

Using a negative lookahead

Finally, if we wanted to use a **negative lookahead**, as in a lookahead group that makes sure that the included text does not follow a pattern, we can simply use an exclamation point instead of an equal to sign:

```
var text = "Mr. Smith & Mrs. Doe";

text.match(/\w+(?!\.)\b/g);
```

This will match all the words that do not end in a period, that is, it will pull out the names from this text:

```
> var text = "Mr. Smith & Mrs. Doe"
  undefined
> text.match(/\w+(?!\.)\b/g);
  ["Smith", "Doe"]
>
```

Summary

In this chapter, we learned how to work with greedy and nongreedy matches. We also learned how to use groups to create more complex regular expressions. While learning how to group a Regex, we also learned about capturing groups, non-capturing groups, and lookahead groups.

In the next chapter, we will implement everything we've learned so far in this book and create a real-world example to match and validate information inputted by a user.

4
Regex in Practice

In the previous two chapters, we covered Regex's syntax in depth, and at this point, have all the pieces required to build a real-world project, which will be the goal of this chapter.

Knowing Regex's syntax allows you to model text patterns, but sometimes coming up with a good reliable pattern can be more difficult, so taking a look at some actual use cases can really help you learn some common design patterns.

So, in this chapter, we will develop a form, and we will explore the following topics:

- Validating a name
- Validating e-mails
- Validating a Twitter username
- Validating passwords
- Validating URLs
- Manipulating text

Regular expressions and form validation

By far, one of the most common uses for regular expressions on the frontend is for use with user submitted forms, so this is what we will be building. The form we will be building will have all the common fields, such as name, e-mail, website, and so on, but we will also experiment with some text processing besides all the validations.

In real-world applications, you usually are not going to implement the parsing and validation code manually. You can create a regular expression and rely on some JavaScript libraries, such as:

- **jQuery validation**: Refer to `http://jqueryvalidation.org/`
- **Parsely.js**: Refer to `http://parsleyjs.org/`

Even the most popular frameworks support the usage of regular expressions with its native validation engine, such as **AngularJS** (refer to `http://www.ng-newsletter.com/posts/validations.html`).

Setting up the form

This demo will be for a site that allows users to create an online bio, and as such, consists of different types of fields. However, before we get into this (since we won't be building a backend to handle the form), we are going to setup some HTML and JavaScript code to catch the form submission and extract/validate the data entered in it.

To keep the code neat, we will create an array with all the validation functions, and a data object where all the final data will be kept.

Here is a basic outline of the HTML code for which we begin by adding fields:

```
<!DOCTYPE HTML>
<html>
    <head>
        <title>Personal Bio Demo</title>
    </head>
    <body>
        <form id="main_form">
            <input type="submit" value="Process" />
        </form>

        <script>
            // js goes here
        </script>
    </body>
</html>
```

Next, we need to write some JavaScript to catch the form and run through the list of functions that we will be writing. If a function returns false, it means that the verification did not pass and we will stop processing the form. In the event where we get through the entire list of functions and no problems arise, we will log out of the console and data object, which contain all the fields we extracted:

```
<script>
    var fns = [];
    var data = {};

    var form = document.getElementById("main_form");

    form.onsubmit = function(e) {
        e.preventDefault();

        data = {};

        for (var i = 0; i < fns.length; i++) {
            if (fns[i]() == false) {
                return;
            }
        }

        console.log("Verified Data: ", data);
    }
</script>
```

The JavaScript starts by creating the two variables I mentioned previously, we then pull the form's object from the DOM and set the submit handler. The submit handler begins by preventing a page from actually submitting, (as we don't have any backend code in this example) and then we go through the list of functions running them one by one.

Validating fields

In this section, we will explore how to validate different types of fields manually, such as name, e-mail, website URL, and so on.

Matching a complete name

To get our feet wet, let's begin with a simple name field. It's something we have gone through briefly in the past, so it should give you an idea of how our system will work. The following code goes inside the script tags, but only after everything we have written so far:

```
function process_name() {
    var field = document.getElementById("name_field");
    var name = field.value;

    var name_pattern = /^(\S+) (\S*) ?\b(\S+)$/;

    if (name_pattern.test(name) === false) {
        alert("Name field is invalid");
        return false;
    }

    var res = name_pattern.exec(name);
    data.first_name = res[1];
    data.last_name = res[3];

    if (res[2].length > 0) {
        data.middle_name = res[2];
    }

    return true;
}

fns.push(process_name);
```

We get the name field in a similar way to how we got the form, then, we extract the value and test it against a pattern to match a full name. If the name doesn't match the pattern, we simply alert the user and return `false` to let the form handler know that the validations have failed. If the name field is in the correct format, we set the corresponding fields on the data object (remember, the middle name is optional here). The last line just adds this function to the array of functions, so it will be called when the form is submitted.

The last thing required to get this working is to add HTML for this form field, so inside the form tags (right before the submit button), you can add this text input:

```
Name: <input type="text" id="name_field" /><br />
```

Opening this page in your browser, you should be able to test it out by entering different values into the **Name** box. If you enter a valid name, you should get the data object printed out with the correct parameters, otherwise you should be able to see this alert message:

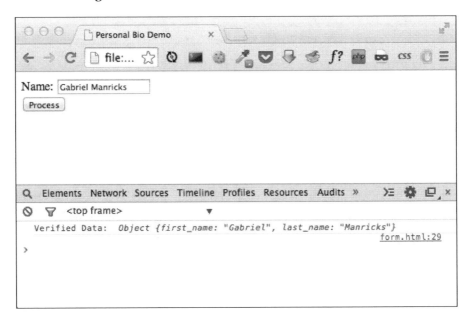

Understanding the complete name Regex

Let's go back to the regular expression used to match the name entered by a user:

```
/^(\S+) (\S*) ?\b(\S+)$/
```

The following is a brief explanation of the Regex:

- The ^ character asserts its position at the beginning of a string
- The first capturing group (\S+)
    - \S+ matches a non-white space character [^\r\n\t\f]
    - The + quantifier between one and unlimited times
- The second capturing group (\S*)
    - \S* matches any non-whitespace character [^\r\n\t\f]
    - The * quantifier between zero and unlimited times

- " ?" matches the whitespace character
  - The ? quantifier between zero and one time
  - \b asserts its position at a (^\w|\w$|\W\w|\w\W) word boundary
- The third capturing group (\S+)
  - \S+ matches a non-whitespace character [^\r\n\t\f]
  - The + quantifier between one and unlimited times
- $ asserts its position at the end of a string

Matching an e-mail with Regex

The next type of field we may want to add is an e-mail field. E-mails may look pretty simple at first glance, but there are a large variety of e-mails out there. You may just think of creating a word@word.word pattern, but the first section can contain many additional characters besides just letters, the domain can be a subdomain, or the suffix could have multiple parts (such as .co.uk for the UK).

Our pattern will simply look for a group of characters that are not spaces or instances where the @ symbol has been used in the first section. We will then want an @ symbol, followed by another set of characters that have at least one period, followed by the suffix, which in itself could contain another suffix. So, this can be accomplished in the following manner:

```
/[^\s@]+@[^\s@.]+\.[^\s@]+/
```

> The pattern of our example is very simple and will not match every valid e-mail address. There is an official standard for an e-mail address's regular expressions called **RFC 5322**. For more information, please read http://www.regular-expressions.info/email.html.

So, let's add the field to our page:

```
Email: <input type="text" id="email_field" /><br />
```

We can then add this function to verify it:

```
function process_email() {
    var field = document.getElementById("email_field");
    var email = field.value;

    var email_pattern = /^[^\s@]+@[^\s@.]+\.[^\s@]+$/;
```

```
    if (email_pattern.test(email) === false) {
        alert("Email is invalid");
        return false;
    }

    data.email = email;
    return true;
}

fns.push(process_email);
```

 There is an HTML5 field type specifically designed for e-mails, but here we are verifying manually, as this is a Regex book. For more information, please refer to http://www.w3.org/TR/html-markup/input. email.html.

Understanding the e-mail Regex

Let's go back to the regular expression used to match the name entered by the user:

```
/^[^\s@]+@[^\s@.]+\.[^\s@]+$/
```

Following is a brief explanation of the Regex:

- ^ asserts a position at the beginning of the string
- [^\s@]+ matches a single character that is not present in the following list:
    - The + quantifier between one and unlimited times
    - \s matches any white space character [\r\n\t\f]
    - @ matches the @ literal character
- [^\s@.]+ matches a single character that is not present in the following list:
    - The + quantifier between one and unlimited times
    - \s matches a [\r\n\t\f] whitespace character
    - @. is a single character in the @. list, literally
    - \. matches the . character literally
- [^\s@]+ match a single character that is not present in the following list:
    - The + quantifier between one and unlimited times
    - \s matches [\r\n\t\f] a whitespace character
    - @ is the @ literal character
- $ asserts its position at end of a string

Matching a Twitter name

The next field we are going to add is a field for a Twitter username. For the unfamiliar, a Twitter username is in the `@username` format, but when people enter this in, they sometimes include the preceding @ symbol and on other occasions, they only write the username by itself. Obviously, internally we would like everything to be stored uniformly, so we will need to extract the username, regardless of the @ symbol, and then manually prepend it with one, so regardless of whether it was there or not, the end result will look the same.

So again, let's add a field for this:

```
Twitter: <input type="text" id="twitter_field" /><br />
```

Now, let's write the function to handle it:

```
function process_twitter() {
    var field = document.getElementById("twitter_field");
    var username = field.value;

    var twitter_pattern = /^@?(\w+)$/;

    if (twitter_pattern.test(username) === false) {
        alert("Twitter username is invalid");
        return false;
    }

    var res = twitter_pattern.exec(username);
    data.twitter = "@" + res[1];
    return true;
}

fns.push(process_twitter);
```

If a user inputs the @ symbol, it will be ignored, as we will add it manually after checking the username.

Understanding the twitter username Regex

Let's go back to the regular expression used to match the name entered by the user:

```
/^@?(\w+)$/
```

This is a brief explanation of the Regex:

- ^ asserts its position at start of the string
- @? matches the @ character, literally
    - The ? quantifier between zero and one time
- First capturing group (\w+)
    - \w+ matches a [a-zA-Z0-9_] word character
    - The + quantifier between one and unlimited times
- $ asserts its position at end of a string

Matching passwords

Another popular field, which can have some unique constraints, is a password field. Now, not every password field is interesting; you may just allow just about anything as a password, as long as the field isn't left blank. However, there are sites where you need to have at least one letter from each case, a number, and at least one other character. Considering all the ways these can be combined, creating a pattern that can validate this could be quite complex. A much better solution for this, and one that allows us to be a bit more verbose with our error messages, is to create four separate patterns and make sure the password matches each of them.

For the input, it's almost identical:

```
Password: <input type="password" id="password_field" /><br />
```

The process_password function is not very different from the previous example as we can see its code as follows:

```
function process_password() {
    var field = document.getElementById("password_field");
    var password = field.value;

    var contains_lowercase = /[a-z]/;
    var contains_uppercase = /[A-Z]/;
    var contains_number = /[0-9]/;
    var contains_other = /[^a-zA-Z0-9]/;

    if (contains_lowercase.test(password) === false) {
        alert("Password must include a lowercase letter");
        return false;
    }
```

```
        if (contains_uppercase.test(password) === false) {
            alert("Password must include an uppercase letter");
            return false;
        }

        if (contains_number.test(password) === false) {
            alert("Password must include a number");
            return false;
        }

        if (contains_other.test(password) === false) {
            alert("Password must include a non-alphanumeric character");
            return false;
        }

        data.password = password;
        return true;
    }

    fns.push(process_password);
```

All in all, you may say that this is a pretty basic validation and something we have already covered, but I think it's a great example of working smart as opposed to working hard. Sure, we probably could have created one long pattern that would check everything together, but it would be less clear and less flexible. So, by breaking it into smaller and more manageable validations, we were able to make clear patterns, and at the same time, improve their usability with more helpful alert messages.

Matching URLs

Next, let's create a field for the user's website; the HTML for this field is:

```
Website: <input type="text" id="website_field" /><br />
```

A URL can have many different protocols, but for this example, let's restrict it to only http or https links. Next, we have the domain name with an optional subdomain, and we need to end it with a suffix. The suffix itself can be a single word, such as .com or it can have multiple segments, such as.co.uk.

All in all, our pattern looks similar to this:

```
/^(?:https?:\/\/)?\w+(?:\.\w+)?(?:\.[A-Z]{2,3})+$/i
```

Here, we are using multiple noncapture groups, both for when sections are optional and for when we want to repeat a segment. You may have also noticed that we are using the case insensitive flag (/i) at the end of the regular expression, as links can be written in lowercase or uppercase.

Now, we'll implement the actual function:

```
function process_website() {
    var field = document.getElementById("website_field");
    var website = field.value;

    var pattern = /^(?:https?:\/\/)?\w+(?:\.\w+)?(?:\.[A-Z]{2,3})+$/i

    if (pattern.test(website) === false) {
        alert("Website is invalid");
        return false;
    }

    data.website = website;
    return true;
}

fns.push(process_website);
```

At this point, you should be pretty familiar with the process of adding fields to our form and adding a function to validate them. So, for our remaining examples let's shift our focus a bit from validating inputs to manipulating data.

Understanding the URL Regex

Let's go back to the regular expression used to match the name entered by the user:

```
/^(?:https?:\/\/)?\w+(?:\.\w+)?(?:\.[A-Z]{2,3})+$/i
```

This is a brief explanation of the Regex:

- ^ asserts its position at start of a string
- (?:https?:\/\/)? is a non-capturing group
    - The ? quantifier between zero and one time
    - http matches the http characters literally (case-insensitive)

- `s?` matches the `s` character literally (case-insensitive)
  - ○ The `?` quantifier between zero and one time
  - ○ `:` matches the `:` character literally
  - ○ `\/` matches the `/` character literally
  - ○ `\/` matches the `/` character literally

- `\w+` matches a `[a-zA-Z0-9_]` word character
  - ○ The `+` quantifier between one and unlimited times

- `(?:\.\w+)?` is a non-capturing group
  - ○ The `?` quantifier between zero and one time
  - ○ `\.` matches the `.` character literally

- `\w+` matches a `[a-zA-Z0-9_]` word character
  - ○ The `+` quantifier between one and unlimited times

- `(?:\.[A-Z]{2,3})+` is a non-capturing group
  - ○ The `+` quantifier between one and unlimited times
  - ○ `\.` matches the `.` character literally

- `[A-Z]{2,3}` matches a single character present in this list
  - ○ The `{2,3}` quantifier between2 and 3 times
  - ○ `A-Z` is a single character in the range between A and Z (case insensitive)

- `$` asserts its position at end of a string
- `i` modifier: insensitive. Case insensitive letters, meaning it will match a-z and A-Z.

Manipulating data

We are going to add one more input to our form, which will be for the user's description. In the description, we will parse for things, such as e-mails, and then create both a plain text and HTML version of the user's description.

The HTML for this form is pretty straightforward; we will be using a standard textbox and give it an appropriate field:

```
Description: <br />
<textarea id="description_field"></textarea><br />
```

Next, let's start with the bare scaffold needed to begin processing the form data:

```
function process_description() {
    var field = document.getElementById("description_field");
    var description = field.value;

    data.text_description = description;

    // More Processing Here

    data.html_description = "<p>" + description + "</p>";

    return true;
}

fns.push(process_description);
```

This code gets the text from the textbox on the page and then saves both a plain text version and an HTML version of it. At this stage, the HTML version is simply the plain text version wrapped between a pair of paragraph tags, but this is what we will be working on now. The first thing I want to do is split between paragraphs, in a text area the user may have different split-ups—lines and paragraphs. For our example, let's say the user just entered a single new line character, then we will add a <br /> tag and if there is more than one character, we will create a new paragraph using the <p> tag.

Using the String.replace method

We are going to use JavaScript's replace method on the string object This function can accept a Regex pattern as its first parameter, and a function as its second; each time it finds the pattern it will call the function and anything returned by the function will be inserted in place of the matched text.

So, for our example, we will be looking for new line characters, and in the function, we will decide if we want to replace the new line with a break line tag or an actual new paragraph, based on how many new line characters it was able to pick up:

```
var line_pattern = /\n+/g;
description = description.replace(line_pattern, function(match) {
    if (match == "\n") {
        return "<br />";
    } else {
        return "</p><p>";
    }
});
```

The first thing you may notice is that we need to use the g flag in the pattern, so that it will look for all possible matches as opposed to only the first. Besides this, the rest is pretty straightforward. Consider this form:

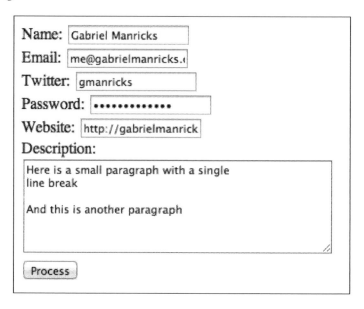

If you take a look at the output from the console of the preceding code, you should get something similar to this:

```
email: "me@gabrielmanricks.com"
first_name: "Gabriel"
html_description: "<p>Here is a small paragraph with a single<br />line break</p><p>And this is another paragraph</p>"
last_name: "Manricks"
password: "passWORD1234!"
text_description: "Here is a small paragraph with a single line break  And this is another paragraph"
twitter: "@gmanricks"
website: "http://gabrielmanricks.com"
```

Matching a description field

The next thing we need to do is try and extract e-mails from the text and automatically wrap them in a link tag. We have already covered a Regexp pattern to capture e-mails, but we will need to modify it slightly, as our previous pattern expects that an e-mail is the only thing present in the text. In this situation, we are interested in all the e-mails included in a large body of text.

If you were simply looking for a word, you would be able to use the \b matcher, which matches any boundary (that can be the end of a word/the end of a sentence), so instead of the dollar sign, which we used before to denote the end of a string, we would place the boundary character to denote the end of a word. However, in our case it isn't quite good enough, as there are boundary characters that are valid e-mail characters, for example, the period character is valid. To get around this, we can use the boundary character in conjunction with a lookahead group and say we want it to end with a word boundary, but only if it is followed by a space or end of a sentence/string. This will ensure we aren't cutting off a subdomain or a part of a domain, if there is some invalid information mid-way through the address.

Now, we aren't creating something that will try and parse e-mails no matter how they are entered; the point of creating validators and patterns is to force the user to enter something logical. That said, we assume that if the user wrote an e-mail address and then a period, that he/she didn't enter an invalid address, rather, he/she entered an address and then ended a sentence (the period is not part of the address).

In our code, we assume that to the end an address, the user is either going to have a space after, such as some kind of punctuation, or that he/she is ending the string/line. We no longer have to deal with lines because we converted them to HTML, but we do have to worry that our pattern doesn't pick up an HTML tag in the process.

At the end of this, our pattern will look similar to this:

```
/\b[^\s<>@]+@[^\s<>@.]+\.[^\s<>@]+\b(?=.?(?:\s|<|$))/g
```

We start off with a word boundary, then, we look for the pattern we had before. I added both the (>) greater-than and the (<) less-than characters to the group of disallowed characters, so that it will not pick up any HTML tags. At the end of the pattern, you can see that we want to end on a word boundary, but only if it is followed by a space, an HTML tag, or the end of a string. The complete function, which does all the matching, is as follows:

```
function process_description() {
    var field = document.getElementById("description_field");
    var description = field.value;

    data.text_description = description;

    var line_pattern = /\n+/g;
    description = description.replace(line_pattern, function(match) {
        if (match == "\n") {
            return "<br />";
        } else {
            return "</p><p>";
```

```
    }
  });

  var email_pattern = /\b[^\s<>@]+@[^\s<>@.]+\.[^\s<>@]+\b(?=.?(?:\
s|<|$))/g;
    description = description.replace(email_pattern, function(match){
      return "<a href='mailto:" + match + "'>" + match + "</a>";
    });

    data.html_description = "<p>" + description + "</p>";

    return true;
}
```

We can continue to add fields, but I think the point has been understood. You have a pattern that matches what you want, and with the extracted data, you are able to extract and manipulate the data into any format you may need.

Understanding the description Regex

Let's go back to the regular expression used to match the name entered by the user:

/\b[^\s<>@]+@[^\s<>@.]+\.[^\s<>@]+\b(?=.?(?:\s|<|$))/g

This is a brief explanation of the Regex:

- \b asserts its position at a (^\w|\w$|\W\w|\w\W) word boundary
- [^\s<>@]+ matches a single character not present in the list:
    - ○ The + quantifier between one and unlimited times
    - ○ \s matches a [\r\n\t\f] whitespace character
    - ○ <>@ is a single character in the <>@ list (case-sensitive)
    - ○ @ matches the @ character literally

- [^\s<>@.]+ matches a single character not present in this list:
    - ○ The + quantifier between one and unlimited times
    - ○ \s matches any [\r\n\t\f] whitespace character
    - ○ <>@. is a single character in the <>@. list literally (case sensitive)
    - ○ \. matches the . character literally

- [^\s<>@]+ matches a single character not present in this the list:
  - ◦ The + quantifier between one and unlimited times
  - ◦ \s matches a [\r\n\t\f] whitespace character
  - ◦ <>@ is a single character in the <>@ list literally (case sensitive)
  - ◦ \b asserts its position at a (^\w|\w$|\W\w|\w\W) word boundary
- (?=.?(?:\s|<|$)) Positive lookahead - Assert that the Regex below can be matched
  - ◦ .? matches any character (except new line)
  - ◦ The ? quantifier between zero and one time
  - ◦ (?:\s|<|$) is a non-capturing group:
- First alternative: \s matches any white space character [\r\n\t\f]
- Second alternative: < matches the character < literally
- Third alternative: $ assert position at end of the string
- The g modifier: global match. Returns all matches of the regular expression, not only the first one

Explaining a Markdown example

More examples of regular expressions can be seen with the popular **Markdown** syntax (refer to http://en.wikipedia.org/wiki/Markdown). This is a situation where a user is forced to write things in a custom format, although it's still a format, which saves typing and is easier to understand. For example, to create a link in Markdown, you would type something similar to this:

```
[Click Me](http://gabrielmanricks.com)
```

This would then be converted to:

```
<a href="http://gabrielmanricks.com">Click Me</a>
```

Disregarding any validation on the URL itself, this can easily be achieved using this pattern:

```
/\[(([^\]]*)\]\(((([^(]*)\)/g
```

It looks a little complex, because both the square brackets and parenthesis are both special characters that need to be escaped. Basically, what we are saying is that we want an open square bracket, anything up to the closing square bracket, then we want an open parenthesis, and again, anything until the closing parenthesis.

A good website to write markdown documents is `http://dillinger.io/`.

Since we wrapped each section into its own capture group, we can write this function:

```
text.replace(/\[(([^\]]*)\]\((([^(]*)\)/g, function(match, text, link){
    return "<a href='" + link + "'>" + text + "</a>";
});
```

We haven't been using capture groups in our manipulation examples, but if you use them, then the first parameter to the callback is the entire match (similar to the ones we have been working with) and then all the individual groups are passed as subsequent parameters, in the order that they appear in the pattern.

Summary

In this chapter, we covered a couple of examples that showed us how to both validate user inputs as well as manipulate them. We also took a look at some common design patterns and saw how it's sometimes better to simplify the problem instead of using brute force in one pattern for the purpose of creating validations.

In the next chapter, we will continue exploring some real-world problems by developing an application with **Node.js**, which can be used to read a file and extract its information, displaying it in a more user friendly manner.

5
Node.js and Regex

So far, we've had fun learning how to create regular expressions for different situations. However, you may be wondering what it would be like to apply a regular expression in a real-world situation, such as reading a log file and presenting its information in a user-friendlier format?

In this chapter, we will learn how to implement a simple **Node.js** application that reads a log file and parses it using a regular expression. This way, we can retrieve specific information from it and output it in a different format. We are going to test all the knowledge we obtained from the previous chapters of this book.

In this chapter we will cover the following topics:

- Installing the required software to develop our example
- Reading a file with Node.js
- Analyzing the anatomy of an Apache log file
- Creating a parse with regular expressions to read an Apache log file

Setting up Node.js

Since we will be developing a Node.js application, the first step is to have Node.js installed. We can get it from `http://nodejs.org/download/`. Just follow the download instructions and we will have it set up on our computer.

 If this is your first time working with Node.js, please go through the tutorials at `https://nodejs.org/`.

To make sure we have Node.js installed, open the terminal application (Command Prompt, if you're using Windows), and type `node -v`. The Node.js version installed should be displayed as follows:

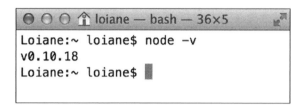

We are now good to go!

Getting started with our application

Let's start developing our sample application with Node.js, which will read a log file and parse its information using a regular expression. We are going to create all the required code inside a JavaScript file, which we will name as `regex.js`. Before we start coding, we will perform a simple test. Add the following content inside the `regex.js`:

```
console.log('Hello, World!');
```

Next, in the terminal application, execute the `regex.js` command node from the directory that the file was created in. The **Hello, World!** message should be displayed as follows:

```
● ○ ○                    regex — bash — 64×5

Loiane:~ loiane$ cd /Applications/XAMPP/xamppfiles/htdocs/regex
Loiane:regex loiane$ node regex.js
Hello, World!
Loiane:regex loiane$ ▊
```

The hello world application with Node.js is created and it works! We can now start coding our application.

Reading a file with Node.js

As the main goal of our application is to read a file, we need the file that the application is going to read! We will be using a sample Apache log file. There are many files on the Internet, but we will be using the log file that can be downloaded from `http://fossies.org/linux/source-highlight/tests/access.log`. Place the file in the same directory that the `regex.js` file was created.

> This sample Apache log file is also available within the source code bundle from this book.

To read a file with Node.js, we need to import the Node.js filesystem module. Remove the `console.log` message we placed inside the `regex.js` file and add the following line of code:

```
var fs = require('fs');
```

> To learn more about the Node.js filesystem module, please read its documentation at `http://nodejs.org/api/fs.html`.

The next step is to open the file and read its content. We are going to use the following code to do this:

```
fs.readFile('access.log', function (err, data) {//#1

  if (err) throw err;//#2

  var text = data.toString();//#3

  var lines = text.split('\n');//#4

  lines.forEach(function(line) {//#5
    console.log(line);//#6
  });
});
```

According to the Node.js documentation, the `readFile` function (#1) can receive three arguments: the name of the file (`access.log`), certain options (that we are not using in this example), and the callback function that will be executed when the contents of the file are loaded in the memory.

To learn more about the `readLine` function, please access `http://nodejs.org/api/fs.html#fs_fs_readfile_filename_options_callback`.

The callback function receives two arguments. The first one is the error. In case something goes wrong, an exception will be thrown (#2). The second argument is `data`, which contains the file contents. We are going to store a string with all the file contents in a variable named `text` (#3).

Each record of the log is then placed in a row of the file. So, we can go ahead and separate the file records and store it into an array (#4). We can now iterate the array that holds the log rows (#5) and perform an action in each line. In this case, we are simply outputting the content of each line in `console` (#6) for now. We will replace line #6 of the code with a different logic in the next section.

If we execute the `regex.js` command node, all the file content should be displayed as follows:

```
● ○ ○                    🗀 regex — bash — 113×23
Loiane:~ loiane$ cd /Applications/XAMPP/xamppfiles/htdocs/regex
Loiane:regex loiane$ node regex.js
127.0.0.1 - jan [30/Jun/2004:22:20:17 +0200] "GET /cgi-bin/trac.cgi/login HTTP/1.1" 302 4370 "http://saturn.solar
_system/cgi-bin/trac.cgi" "Mozilla/5.0 (X11; U; Linux i686; en-US; rv:1.7) Gecko/20040620 Galeon/1.3.15"
127.0.0.1 - - [01/Jun/2004:20:57:40 +0200] "GET / HTTP/1.1" 200 1456 "-" "Mozilla/5.0 (X11; U; Linux i686; en-US;
 rv:1.6) Gecko/20040517 Galeon/1.3.14"
127.0.0.1 - - [01/Jun/2004:20:57:40 +0200] "GET /apache_pb.gif HTTP/1.1" 200 2326 "http://localhost/" "Mozilla/5.
0 (X11; U; Linux i686; en-US; rv:1.6) Gecko/20040517 Galeon/1.3.14"
127.0.0.1 - - [01/Jun/2004:20:57:43 +0200] "GET /manual/ HTTP/1.1" 404 65 "http://localhost/" "Mozilla/5.0 (X11;
U; Linux i686; en-US; rv:1.6) Gecko/20040517 Galeon/1.3.14"
127.0.0.1 - - [01/Jun/2004:20:57:47 +0200] "GET / HTTP/1.1" 200 1456 "-" "Mozilla/5.0 (X11; U; Linux i686; en-US;
 rv:1.6) Gecko/20040517 Galeon/1.3.14"
127.0.0.1 - - [01/Jun/2004:21:02:11 +0200] "GET / HTTP/1.1" 200 1456 "-" "Mozilla/5.0 (X11; U; Linux i686; en-US;
 rv:1.6) Gecko/20040517 Galeon/1.3.14"
127.0.0.1 - - [01/Jun/2004:21:02:11 +0200] "GET /apache_pb.gif HTTP/1.1" 200 2326 "http://localhost/" "Mozilla/5.
0 (X11; U; Linux i686; en-US; rv:1.6) Gecko/20040517 Galeon/1.3.14"
127.0.0.1 - - [01/Jun/2004:21:02:13 +0200] "GET /manual/ HTTP/1.1" 404 79 "http://localhost/" "Mozilla/5.0 (X11;
U; Linux i686; en-US; rv:1.6) Gecko/20040517 Galeon/1.3.14"
127.0.0.1 - - [01/Jun/2004:21:02:14 +0200] "GET /manual/ HTTP/1.1" 404 79 "http://localhost/" "Mozilla/5.0 (X11;
U; Linux i686; en-US; rv:1.6) Gecko/20040517 Galeon/1.3.14"
127.0.0.1 - - [01/Jun/2004:21:02:17 +0200] "GET /manual/ HTTP/1.1" 404 79 "http://localhost/" "Mozilla/5.0 (X11;
U; Linux i686; en-US; rv:1.6) Gecko/20040517 Galeon/1.3.14"
127.0.0.1 - - [01/Jun/2004:21:03:19 +0200] "GET / HTTP/1.0" 200 1456 "-" "Links (2.1pre11; Linux 2.6.5-gentoo-r1
```

The anatomy of an Apache log file

Before we create the regular expression that will match a line of the Apache file, we need to understand what kind of information it holds.

Let's take a look at a line from `access.log`:

```
127.0.0.1 - jan [30/Jun/2004:22:20:17 +0200] "GET /cgi-bin/trac.cgi/
login HTTP/1.1" 302 4370 "http://saturn.solar_system/cgi-bin/trac.
cgi" "Mozilla/5.0 (X11; U; Linux i686; en-US; rv:1.7) Gecko/20040620
Galeon/1.3.15"
```

The Apache access log that we are reading follows the `%h %l %u %t \"%r\" %>s %b \"%{Referer}i\" \"%{User-agent}i\"` format. Let's take a look at each part:

- `%h`: The first part of the log is the (`127.0.0.1`) IP address
- `%l`: In the second part, the hyphen in the output indicates that the requested piece of information is not available
- `%u`: The third part is the user ID of the person requesting the (`jan`) document.
- `%t`: The fourth part is the time taken for the request to be received, such as (`[30/Jun/2004:22:20:17 +0200]`). It is in the `[day/month/ year:hour:minute:second zone]` format, where:
  - day = 2*digit
  - `month` = 3*letter
  - `year` = 4*digit
  - `hour` = 2*digit
  - `minute` = 2*digit
  - `second` = 2*digit
  - `zone` = (`` `+' `` | `` `-' ``) 4*digit
- `\"%r\"`: The fifth part is the request line from the client that is given in double quotes, such as (`"GET /cgi-bin/trac.cgi/login HTTP/1.1"`)
- `%>s`: The sixth part is the status code that the server sends back to the (`302`) client
- `%b`: The seventh part is the size of the object returned to the (`4370`) client
- `\"%{Referer}i\"`: The eighth part is the site that the client reports having been referred from, which is given in double quotes, such as (`"http:// saturn.solar_system/cgi-bin/trac.cgi"`)
- `\"%{User-agent}i\"`: The ninth and last part is the user-agent HTTP request header and is also given in double quotes, such as (`"Mozilla/5.0 (X11; U; Linux i686; en-US; rv:1.7) Gecko/20040620 Galeon/1.3.15"`)

All the parts are separated by a space. With this information and that given previously, we can start creating our regular expression.

For more information about the format of Apache logs, please read `http://httpd.apache.org/docs/2.2/logs.html`.

Creating the Apache log Regex

In the Apache access log file, we have nine parts that we want to recognize and extract from each line of the file. We can try two approaches while creating a Regex: we can be very specific or more generic. As mentioned previously, the most powerful regular expressions are the ones that are generic. We will try to achieve these expressions in this chapter as well.

For example, for the first part of the log, we know it is an IP address. We can be specific and use a Regex for the (`^\b\d{1,3}\.\d{1,3}\.\d{1,3}\.\d{1,3}\b`) IPs or, as we know, the log starts with an IP we can use, such as `^(\S+)`, where, `^` means it matches the beginning of the input and `\s` matches a single character other than whitespace. The `^(\S+)` expression will match exactly the first part of the log, which consists of some specific information until it finds a space (such as the IP address). Also, `^(\S+)` is simpler than using `^\b\d{1,3}\.\d{1,3}\.\d{1,3}\.\d{1,3}\b` and we've still achieved the same result.

Let's go ahead and test the regular expression created so far:

```
/^(\S+)/.exec('127.0.0.1 - jan [30/Jun/2004:22:20:17 +0200] "GET /cgi-
bin/trac.cgi/login HTTP/1.1" 302 4370 "http://saturn.solar_system/cgi-
bin/trac.cgi" "Mozilla/5.0 (X11; U; Linux i686; en-US; rv:1.7) Gecko/20040620
Galeon/1.3.15"');
["127.0.0.1", "127.0.0.1"]
```

To recapitulate what we learned in *Chapter 1, Getting Started with Regex,* the `exec` method executes a search for a match in a string. It returns an array of information, as it is the first position the string has matched and then the subsequent position in each part of the Regex.

For the second and third parts, we can continue using the `^(\S+)` Regex. The second and third part can contain certain information (including a set of alphanumeric characters), or it can contain a hyphen. We are interested in the information present in each part until it finds a space. So, we can add two more `^(\S+)` to our Regex: `^(\S+) (\S+) (\S+)` and test it:

```
/^(\S+) (\S+) (\S+)/.exec('127.0.0.1 - jan [30/Jun/2004:22:20:17 +0200] "GET
/cgi-bin/trac.cgi/login HTTP/1.1" 302 4370 "http://saturn.solar_system/cgi-
bin/trac.cgi" "Mozilla/5.0 (X11; U; Linux i686; en-US; rv:1.7) Gecko/20040620
Galeon/1.3.15"');
["127.0.0.1 - jan", "127.0.0.1", "-", "jan"]
```

The first three parts of the log line are recognized.

Creating a Regex for the time part

The fourth part is the time that is given between brackets. The Regex that is going to match the time from the log is \[([^:]+):(\d+:\d+:\d+) ([^\]]+)\].

Let's see how we can achieve this result.

First, we have the opening and closing brackets. We cannot simply use [] as part of the Regex, because brackets in a regular expression represent a set of characters (groups as we learned in *Chapter 3, Special Characters*). So, we need to use the (\) scape character before each bracket, so that we can represent the bracket as part of the regular expression.

The next piece of the time Regex is "([^:]+):". After the opening bracket, we want to match any character until we find the (:) colon. We learned in *Chapter 2, The Basics* about a negated range and this is exactly what we are going to use. We are expecting any character to be present except the colon, so we use [^:] to represent it. Also, it can consist of one or more characters, such as (+). Next, we are expecting a (:) colon. With this piece of the regular expression, we can match "[30/Jun/2004:" from "[30/Jun/2004:22:20:17 +0200]".

The same Regex can be represented as "(\d{2}\/\w{3}\/\d{4}):", since the day is given in the form of two digits, the month is given in three characters, and the year in four digits, and are separated by \.

The next piece of the Regex is (\d+:\d+:\d+). It will match 22:20:17 from the example. The \d character matches any number (+ matches one or more), followed by a (:) colon. We could also use (\d{2}:\d{2}:\d{2}), since the hours, minutes, and seconds are represented by two digits each.

The final piece is ([^\]]+)\]. We are expecting any character except "]" ([^\]] – negate]). This will match the time zone (+0200). We could also use ([\+|-]\d{4}) as Regex, since the zone format is + or -, followed by four digits.

When we test the regular expression, we will get this:

```
/^(\S+) (\S+) (\S+) \[(\d{2}\/\w{3}\/\d{4}):(\d{2}:\d{2}:\d{2}) ([\+|-
]\d{4})\]/.exec('127.0.0.1 - jan [30/Jun/2004:22:20:17 +0200] "GET /cgi-
bin/trac.cgi/login HTTP/1.1" 302 4370 "http://saturn.solar_system/cgi-
bin/trac.cgi" "Mozilla/5.0 (X11; U; Linux i686; en-US; rv:1.7) Gecko/20040620
Galeon/1.3.15"');
["127.0.0.1 - jan [30/Jun/2004:22:20:17 +0200]", "127.0.0.1", "-", "jan",
"30/Jun/2004", "22:20:17", "+0200"]
```

Note that each piece of the time was split (the date, time, and zone) by a subset, separated by a parenthesis group "()". If we want to have the time as a single piece, we can remove the subsets: \ [(\d{2}\/\w{3}\/\d{4}:\d{2}:\d{2}:\d{2} [\+|-]\ d{4})\].

Creating a Regex for the request information

Following the parts that we separated (in a few sections previous to this one), let's work on the fifth part of the log, which is the request information.

Let's take a look at the "GET /cgi-bin/trac.cgi/login HTTP/1.1" example, so we can create a regular expression from it.

The request is given in double quotes, so that we know a regular expression is to be created inside \" \". From the preceding example, there are three pieces (GET, / cgi-bin/trac.cgi/login, and HTTP/1.1). So, GET can be represented by (\S+).

Next, we have /cgi-bin/trac.cgi/login. We will use (.*?), meaning, it can be any character or nothing else. We will use this because we do not know the format of this information.

Then, we have the HTTP/1.1 protocol and to match it, we will also use (\S+).

This will be the result when we try to match the regular expression:

```
/^(\S+) (\S+) (\S+) \[(\d{2}\/\w{3}\/\d{4}:\d{2}:\d{2}:\d{2} [\+|-]\d{4})\] \"
(\S+ .*? \S+)\"/.exec('127.0.0.1 - jan [30/Jun/2004:22:20:17 +0200] "GET /cgi-
bin/trac.cgi/login HTTP/1.1" 302 4370 "http://saturn.solar_system/cgi-
bin/trac.cgi" "Mozilla/5.0 (X11; U; Linux i686; en-US; rv:1.7) Gecko/20040620
Galeon/1.3.15"');
["127.0.0.1 - jan [30/Jun/2004:22:20:17 +0200] "GET /cgi-bin/trac.cgi/login
HTTP/1.1"", "127.0.0.1", "-", "jan", "30/Jun/2004:22:20:17 +0200", "GET /cgi-
bin/trac.cgi/login HTTP/1.1"]
```

If we want to retrieve each part of the request separately (such as the method, resource, and protocol), we can use (), as we used in the first approach, for the time.

Creating a Regex for the status code and object size

The next two parts of the log are simple. The first one is the status, which is represented by 2xx, 3xx, 4xx, or 5xx, so, it is basically three digits. We can represent it in two ways: (\S+), which will match any character until it finds a space, or (\d{3}). Of course, we can be even more specific and allow the first digit to be only 2, 3, 4, or 5, though, let's not complicate it any more than is needed.

A number can also represent the object size. However, if no information is returned, it will be represented by a hyphen, so (\S+) represents best. Or we can also use ([\d|-]+).

The output will be the following:

```
/^(\S+) (\S+) (\S+) \[(\d{2}\/\w{3}\/\d{4}:\d{2}:\d{2}:\d{2} [\+|-]\d{4})\] \"
(\S+ .*? \S+)\" (\d{3}) ([\d|-]+)/.exec('127.0.0.1 — jan [30/Jun/2004:22:20:17
+0200] "GET /cgi-bin/trac.cgi/login HTTP/1.1" 302 4370
"http://saturn.solar_system/cgi-bin/trac.cgi" "Mozilla/5.0 (X11; U; Linux i686;
en-US; rv:1.7) Gecko/20040620 Galeon/1.3.15"');
["127.0.0.1 — jan [30/Jun/2004:22:20:17 +0200] "GET /cgi-bin/trac.cgi/login
HTTP/1.1" 302 4370", "127.0.0.1", "—", "jan", "30/Jun/2004:22:20:17 +0200",
"GET /cgi-bin/trac.cgi/login HTTP/1.1", "302", "4370"]
```

Creating a Regex for the referrer and the user agent

Both parts are given in double quotes. We can represent the information using the "([^"]*)" expression, which means including any character except ". We can apply it in both parts.

With the addition of the last two parts of the log, we will get this output:

```
/^(\S+) (\S+) (\S+) \[(\d{2}\/\w{3}\/\d{4}:\d{2}:\d{2}:\d{2} [\+|-]\d{4})\] \"
(\S+ .*? \S+)\" (\d{3}) ([\d|-]+) "([^"]*)" "([^"]*)"/.exec('127.0.0.1 — jan
[30/Jun/2004:22:20:17 +0200] "GET /cgi-bin/trac.cgi/login HTTP/1.1" 302 4370
"http://saturn.solar_system/cgi-bin/trac.cgi" "Mozilla/5.0 (X11; U; Linux i686;
en-US; rv:1.7) Gecko/20040620 Galeon/1.3.15"');
["127.0.0.1 — jan [30/Jun/2004:22:20:17 +0200] "GET /cgi-bin/trac.cgi/login
HTTP/1.1" 302 4370 "http://saturn.solar_system/cgi-bin/trac.cgi" "Mozilla/5.0
(X11; U; Linux i686; en-US; rv:1.7) Gecko/20040620 Galeon/1.3.15"",
"127.0.0.1", "—", "jan", "30/Jun/2004:22:20:17 +0200", "GET /cgi-
bin/trac.cgi/login HTTP/1.1", "302", "4370", "http://saturn.solar_system/cgi-
bin/trac.cgi", "Mozilla/5.0 (X11; U; Linux i686; en-US; rv:1.7) Gecko/20040620
Galeon/1.3.15"]
```

Our final Regex to match a line of the Apache access log, is given here:

```
^(\S+) (\S+) (\S+) \[(\d{2}\/\w{3}\/\d{4}:\d{2}:\d{2}:\d{2} [\+|-]\
d{4})\] \"(\S+ .*? \S+)\" (\d{3}) ([\d|-]+) "([^"]*)" "([^"]*)"
```

Trying to create a regular expression at once can be tricky and complicated. However, we've split each part and created a Regex. At the end of all this, all we have to do is combine all these parts together.

We are now ready to continue coding our application.

Parsing each Apache log row

We now know the regular expression that we want to use, so all we need to do is add the (#1) Regex to the code, execute the Regex with each line (#2), and obtain the results (#3). We will simply output the results in the console for now (#4). The code is presented here:

```
var fs = require('fs');

fs.readFile('access.log', function (err, logData) {

  if (err) throw err;

  var text = logData.toString(),
    lines = text.split('\n'),
    results = {},
    regex = /^(\S+) (\S+) (\S+) \[(\d{2}\/\w{3}\/\d{4}:\d{2}:\
d{2}:\d{2} [\+|-]\d{4})\] \"(\S+ .*? \S+)\" (\d{3}) ([\d|-]+)
"([^"]*)" "([^"]*)"/; //#1

  lines.forEach(function(line) {

    results = regex.exec(line); //#2

    for (i=0; i<results.length; i++){ //#3
      console.log(results[i]); //#4
    }

  }); //#5
});
```

Is this the only way of making Regex work with Node.js?

In this example, we used the JavaScript Regex, which we've learned throughout this book. However, Node.js has other packages that can make our lives easier when working with regular expressions. The node-regexp package is one of the packages that provides a new way of working with regular expressions while working with Node.js. It is worth taking a look at it and spending some time playing with it at https://www.npmjs.com/package/node-regexp.

We will continue completing our code in the next two sections.

Creating a JSON object for each row

Let's try to do something more useful with each row of the Apache log. We are going to create a **JavaScript Object Notation (JSON)** object with each row and add it to an array. To wrap our application, we will save the JSON content into a file.

 To learn more about JSON, please refer to http://www.json.org/.

So after the Regex declaration (which is inside the var declaration), we are going to add a new variable that will hold the collection of **JSON** objects we are going to create:

```
jsonObject = [],
row;
```

Instead of lines #3 and #4, as seen in the code of the previous section, we will place this code:

```
if (results){
  row = {
    ip: results[1],
    available: results[2],
    userid: results[3],
    time: results[4],
    request: results[5],
    status: results[6],
    size: results[7],
    referrer: results[8],
    userAgent: results[9],
  }

  jsonObject.push(row);
}
```

This code will verify if any result arises from the execution of the Regex, and will create a JSON object called **row**. Then, we simply need to add the JSON object into the `jsonObject` array.

Next, we will construct the last piece of the Node.js application. We will create a JSON file with the JSON array that we created. We need to place the following code in the #5 line of the code, as seen in the previous section:

```
var outputFilename = 'log.json';
fs.writeFile(outputFilename, JSON.stringify(jsonObject, null, 4),
  function(err) {
  if(err) {
    console.log(err);
  } else {
    console.log("JSON saved to " + outputFilename);
  }
});
```

 To learn more about the `writeFile` function, please refer to `http://nodejs.org/api/fs.html#fs_fs_writefile_filename_data_options_callback`.

The result will be a JSON with content similar to the following:

```
[
  {
    "ip": "127.0.0.1",
    "available": "-",
    "userid": "jan",
    "time": "30/Jun/2004:22:20:17 +0200",
    "request": "GET /cgi-bin/trac.cgi/login HTTP/1.1",
    "status": "302",
    "size": "4370",
    "referrer": "http://saturn.solar_system/cgi-bin/trac.cgi",
    "userAgent": "Mozilla/5.0 (X11; U; Linux i686; en-US; rv:1.7)
      Gecko/20040620 Galeon/1.3.15"
  }
  //more content
]
```

Display the JSON in a table

The last step is to create a simple HTML page to display the Apache log content. We are going to create an HTML file and place the following code in it:

```html
<!DOCTYPE html>
<html lang="en">
  <head>
    <title>Log</title>
    <link rel="stylesheet" href="http://netdna.bootstrapcdn.com/
bootstrap/3.0.3/css/bootstrap.min.css">
    <link rel="stylesheet" href="https://cdnjs.cloudflare.com/ajax/
libs/bootstrap-table/1.5.0/bootstrap-table.min.css">
    <script src="http://cdnjs.cloudflare.com/ajax/libs/jquery/2.0.3/
jquery.min.js"></script>
    <script src="https://cdnjs.cloudflare.com/ajax/libs/bootstrap-
table/1.5.0/bootstrap-table.min.js"></script>
    <style>
      body{
        margin-top: 30px;
        margin-right: 30px;
        margin-left: 30px;
      }
    </style>
  </head>
```

The preceding code contains the required JavaScript and CSS imports, so that we can display the Apache log.

> The table for this example was created using a Bootstrap table. For more information on its usage and examples, please access http://wenzhixin.net.cn/p/bootstrap-table/docs/examples.html.

The next and last piece of code is the body of the HTML:

```html
<body>
  <table data-toggle="table" data-url="log.json"
    data-cache="false" data-height="400"
    data-show-refresh="true" data-show-toggle="true"
    data-show-columns="true" data-search="true"
    data-select-item-name="toolbar1" >
    <thead>
```

```
        <tr>
          <th data-field="ip">IP</th>
          <th data-field="time">Time</th>
          <th data-field="request">Request Info</th>
          <th data-field="status">Status</th>
          <th data-field="size">Size</th>
          <th data-field="referrer">Referrer</th>
          <th data-field="userAgent">User Agent</th>
        </tr>
      </thead>
    </table>
  </body>
</html>
```

The body will hold a table that will read the content of the log.json file, parse it, and display it.

To be able to open the html file in the browser, we need a server. This is because our code is using an Ajax request to load the JSON file created by the Node.js application. Since we have Node.js installed, we can use its simplest server to execute our code.

In the terminal, execute the following command to install the server:

`npm install http-server -g`

Then, change the directory to the one you created for the HTML file:

`cd chapter05`

Finally, start the server:

`http-server`

You will be able to see the results from the http://localhost:8080/ URL. We can see the final result in the following image:

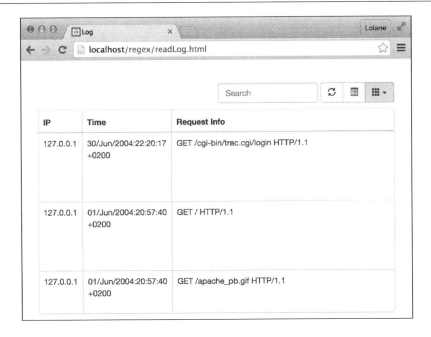

We can also toggle the results in the table and view the complete data:

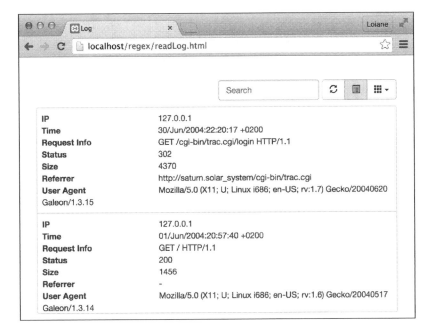

Now we are done with our sample Node.js application, which has read and parsed an Apache log file and can be displayed in a friendlier way.

Summary

In this chapter, we learned how to create a simple Node.js application that read an Apache log file and extracted the log information using a regular expression. We were able to put in to practice the knowledge we acquired in the previous chapters of the book.

We also learned that to create a very complex Regex, it is best to do it in parts. We learned that we can be very specific while creating a regular expression or we can be more generic and achieve the same results.

As a new version of **EcmaScript** is being created (EcmaScript 6, which will add lots of new features to JavaScript), it is good to familiarize yourself with the improvements related to regular expressions as well. For more information please visit http://www.ecmascript.org/dev.php.

We hope you enjoy the book! Have fun creating regular expressions!

JavaScript Regex Cheat Sheet

In this appendix, you can find a summary of the patterns used in regular expressions in JavaScript along with their descriptions, and a list of useful methods to test and create regular expressions.

The following Regex topics will be covered in this appendix:

- Character classes and literals
- Character sets
- Boundaries and quantifiers
- Grouping, alternation, and back reference
- Useful methods

Character classes

In the following table, you can find the patterns for character classes, which tell the Regex to match a single character:

Pattern	Description	Example
.	This matches any character, except newline or another unicode line terminator, such as (\n, \r, \u2028 or \u2029).	/f.o/ matches "fao", "feo", and "foo"
\w	This matches any alphanumeric character, including the underscore. It is equivalent to [a-zA-Z0-9_].	/\w/ matches "f" in "foo"
\W	This matches any single nonword character. It is equivalent to [^a-zA-Z0-9_].	/\W/ matches "%"in "100%"

Pattern	Description	Example
\d	This matches any single digit. It is equivalent to [0-9].	/\d/ matches "1" in "100"
\D	This matches any non digit. It is equivalent to [^0-9].	/\D/ matches "R" in "R2-D2"
\s	This matches any single space character. It is equivalent to [\t\r\n\v\f].	/\s/ matches " " in "foo bar"
\S	This matches any single nonspace character. It is equivalent to [^ \t\r\n\v\f].	/\S/ matches "foo" in "foo bar"

Literals

In the following table, you can find the patterns for literal characters, which tell the Regex to match a special character:

Pattern	Description	Example
Alphanumeric	These match themselves literally.	/javascript book/ matches "javascript book" in "javascript book"
\0	This matches a NUL character.	
\n	This matches a newline character.	
\f	This matches a form feed character.	
\r	This matches a carriage return character.	
\t	This matches a tab character.	
\v	This matches a vertical tab character.	
[\b]	This matches a backspace character.	
\xxx	This matches the ASCII character, expressed by the xxx octal number.	/112/ matches the "J" character
\xdd	This matches the ASCII character, expressed by the dd hex number.	/x4A/ matches the "J" character
\uxxxx	This matches the ASCII character, expressed by the xxxx UNICODE.	/u0237/ matches the "J" character
\	This indicates whether the next character is special and is not to be interpreted literally.	/\^/ matches "^" in "char ^"

Character sets

In the following table, you can find the patterns for character sets, which tell the Regex to match only one character out of several characters.

Pattern	Description	Example
[xyz]	This matches any one character enclosed in the character set. You can use a hyphen to denote the range. For example, / [a-z] / matches any letter in the alphabet and matches / [0-9] / to any single digit.	/ [ao] / matches "a" in "bar"
[^xyz]	This matches any one character, which is not enclosed in the character set.	/ [^ao] / matches "b" in "bar"

Boundaries

In the following table, you can find the patterns for boundaries, which will tell the Regex what position to do the matching in.

Pattern	Description	Example
^	This matches the beginning of an input. If the multiline flag is set to true, it also matches immediately after the (\n) line break character.	/^ The/ matches "The" in "The stars", but not "In The stars".
$	This matches the end of an input. If the multiline flag is set to true, it also matches immediately before the (\n) line break character.	/and$/ matches "and" in "land", but not "and the bar".
\b	This matches any word boundary (test characters must exist at the beginning or at the end of a word within the string).	/va\b/ matches "va" in "this is a java script book", but not "this is a javascript book".
\B	This matches any non-word boundary.	/va\B/ matches "va" in "this is a JavaScript book", but not "this is a JavaScript book".

Grouping, alternation, and back reference

In the following table, you can find the patterns for grouping, alternation, and back reference. The grouping is used to group a set of characters in a Regex. The alternation is used to combine characters into a single regular expression, and the back reference is used to match the same text as previously matched by a capturing group:

Pattern	Description	Example
(x)	This groups characters together to create a clause, that is, it matches x and remembers the match. These are called capturing parentheses.	/(foo)/ matches and remembers "foo" in "foo bar".
()	Parenthesis also serves to capture the desired subpattern within a pattern.	/(\d\d)\/(\d\d)\/(\d\d\d\d)/ matches "12", "12", and "2000" in "12/12/2000".
(?:x)	This matches x but does not capture it. In other words, no numbered references are created for the items within the parenthesis. These are called non-capturing parentheses.	/(?:foo)/ matches, but does not remember "foo" in "foo bar".
|	Alternation combines clauses into one regular expression, and then matches any of the individual clauses. x|y matches either x or y. It is similar to the "OR" statement.	/morning|night/ matches "morning" in "good morning" and matches "night" in "good night".
()\n	"\n" (where n is a number from 1-9) when added to the end of a regular expression pattern, allows you to back reference a subpattern within the pattern, so, the value of the subpattern is remembered and used as part of the matching.	/(no)\1/ matches "nono" in "nono". "\1" is replaced with the value of the first subpattern within the pattern, or (no), to form the final pattern.

Quantifiers

In the following table, you can find the patterns for quantifiers, which specify how many instances of a character, group, or character class must be present in an input for a match to be found.

Pattern	Description	Example
{n}	This matches exactly n occurrences of a regular expression.	/\d{5}/ matches "12345" (five digits) in "1234567890".
{n, }	This matches n or more occurrences of a regular expression.	/\d{5,}/ matches "1234567890" (minimum of five digits) in "1234567890".
{n,m}	This matches n to m number of occurrences of a regular expression.	/\d{5,7}/ matches "1234567" (minimum of five digits and a maximum of seven digits) in "1234567890".
*	This matches zero or more occurrences and is equivalent to {0,}.	/fo*/ matches "foo" in "foo" and matches "fooooooo" in "foooooooooled".
+	This matches one or more occurrences and is equivalent to {1,}.	/o+/ matches "oo" in "foo".
?	This matches zero or one occurrences and is equivalent to {0,1}.	/fo?/ matches "fo" in "foo" and matches "f" in "fairy".
+? *?	"?" can also be used following one of the *, +, ?, or {} quantifiers to make the later match nongreedy, or the minimum number of times versus the default maximum.	/\d{2,4}?/ matches "12" in the "12345" string, instead of "1234" due to "?" at the end of the quantifier nongreedy.
x(?=y)	Positive lookahead: It matches x only if it's followed by y. Note that y is not included as part of the match, acting only as a required condition.	/Java(?=Script|Hut)/ matches "Java" in "JavaScript" or "JavaHut", but not "JavaLand".
x(?!y)	Negative lookahead: It matches x only if it's not followed by y. Note that y is not included as part of the match, acting only as a required condition.	/^\d+(?! years)/ matches "5" in "5 days" or "5 books", but not "5 years".

JavaScript regular expressions methods

In the following table, you can find the methods used to match or test a regular expression. The main JavaScript objects used in regular expressions are `String` and `RegExp`, which represent a pattern (such as `regular expression`).

Method	Description	Example

`String.match(regular expression)`	This executes a search for a match within a string, based on a regular expression.	`var myString = "today is 12-12-2000";`
		
		`var matches = myString.match(/\d{4}/);`
		
		`//returns array ["2000"]`

`RegExp.exec(string)`	This executes a search for a match in its string parameter. Unlike `String.match`, the parameter entered should be a string, not a regular expression pattern.	`var pattern = /\d{4}/;`
		
		`pattern.exec("today is 12-12-2000");`
		
		`//returns array ["2000"]`

`String.replace(regular expression, replacement text)`	This searches and replaces the regular expression portion (match) with the replaced text instead.	`var phone = "(201) 123-4567";`
		
		`var phoneFormatted = phone.replace(/[\(\)-\s]/g, "");`
		
		`//returns 2011234567 (removed ( ) - and blank space)`

`String.split (string literal or regular expression)`	This breaks up a string into an array of substrings, based on a regular expression or fixed string.	`var oldstring = "1,2, 3, 4,   5";`
		
		`var newstring = oldstring.split(/\s*,\s*/);`
		
		`//returns the array ["1","2","3","4","5"]`

`String.search(regular expression)`	This tests for a match in a string. It returns the index of the match, or -1, if it's not found.	`var myString = "today is 12-12-2000";`
		
		`myString.search(/\d{4}/);`
		
		`//returns 15 - index of 2000`

Method	Description	Example

`RegExp.test(string)`	This tests whether the given string matches the Regexp, and returns true if it's matching, and false, if not.	`var pattern = /\d{4}/;`
		`pattern.test("today is 12-12-2000");`
		`//returns true`

In this appendix, we very briefly covered the patterns learned throughout this book in a format that is easy to consult on a day-to-day basis.

Index

W

whitespace character
  matching 34
wildcard character 20
word boundaries
  matching 33
word character 21
writeFile function
  URL 72

X

XML
  about 38
  file, analyzing 3

Thank you for buying
JavaScript Regular Expressions

About Packt Publishing

Packt, pronounced 'packed', published its first book, *Mastering phpMyAdmin for Effective MySQL Management*, in April 2004, and subsequently continued to specialize in publishing highly focused books on specific technologies and solutions.

Our books and publications share the experiences of your fellow IT professionals in adapting and customizing today's systems, applications, and frameworks. Our solution-based books give you the knowledge and power to customize the software and technologies you're using to get the job done. Packt books are more specific and less general than the IT books you have seen in the past. Our unique business model allows us to bring you more focused information, giving you more of what you need to know, and less of what you don't.

Packt is a modern yet unique publishing company that focuses on producing quality, cutting-edge books for communities of developers, administrators, and newbies alike. For more information, please visit our website at www.packtpub.com.

About Packt Open Source

In 2010, Packt launched two new brands, Packt Open Source and Packt Enterprise, in order to continue its focus on specialization. This book is part of the Packt Open Source brand, home to books published on software built around open source licenses, and offering information to anybody from advanced developers to budding web designers. The Open Source brand also runs Packt's Open Source Royalty Scheme, by which Packt gives a royalty to each open source project about whose software a book is sold.

Writing for Packt

We welcome all inquiries from people who are interested in authoring. Book proposals should be sent to author@packtpub.com. If your book idea is still at an early stage and you would like to discuss it first before writing a formal book proposal, then please contact us; one of our commissioning editors will get in touch with you.

We're not just looking for published authors; if you have strong technical skills but no writing experience, our experienced editors can help you develop a writing career, or simply get some additional reward for your expertise.

JavaScript and JSON Essentials

ISBN: 978-1-78328-603-4   Paperback: 120 pages

Successfully build advanced JSON-fueled web applications with this practical, hands-on guide

1. Deploy JSON across various domains.

2. Facilitate metadata storage with JSON.

3. Build a practical data-driven web application with JSON.

Object-Oriented JavaScript
Second Edition

ISBN: 978-1-84969-312-7   Paperback: 382 pages

Learn everything you need to know about OOJS in this comprehensive guide

1. Think in JavaScript.

2. Make object-oriented programming accessible and understandable to web developers.

3. Apply design patterns to solve JavaScript coding problems.

4. Learn coding patterns that unleash the unique power of the language.

Please check **www.PacktPub.com** for information on our titles

Mastering JavaScript
Design Patterns

Mastering JavaScript Design Patterns

ISBN: 978-1-78398-798-6   Paperback: 290 pages

Discover how to use JavaScript design patterns to create powerful applications with reliable and maintainable code

1. Learn how to use tried and true software design methodologies to enhance your Javascript code.

2. Discover robust JavaScript implementations of classic as well as advanced design patterns.

3. Packed with easy-to-follow examples that can be used to create reusable code and extensible designs.

JavaScript Unit Testing

JavaScript Unit Testing

ISBN: 978-178216-062-5   Paperback: 190 pages

Your comprehensive and practical guide to efficiently performing and automating JavaScript unit testing

1. Learn and understand, using practical examples, synchronous and asynchronous JavaScript unit testing.

2. Cover the most popular JavaScript Unit Testing Frameworks including Jasmine, YUITest, QUnit, and JsTestDriver.

3. Automate and integrate your JavaScript Unit Testing for ease and efficiency.

Please check **www.PacktPub.com** for information on our titles

Made in the USA
San Bernardino, CA
30 November 2016